ANDREW
KARL ER

Decisi
and C

A Study o
Norwegia

Universitet
Oslo – Bergen –

For our parents,
MARGARET COOK COWART AND
DEWITT TALMADGE COWART
and
KIRSTEN BROFOSS and ERIK BROFOSS
who, during times past, never
hesitated to review our own
adolescent budgeting decisions
with a tenacity which would
surely have been the envy of
today's government budget
reviewers.

© The Norwegian Research Council for Science and
the Humanities (Norges almenvitenskapelige forskningsråd) 1979
Section B.40.29.014T

Cover design: Oddvar Wold

ISBN 82-00-01882-2

Printed in Norway by
Tangen-Trykk, Drammen

Distribution offices:
NORWAY
Universitetsforlaget
P.O.Box 2977, Tøyen
Oslo 6

UNITED KINGDOM
Global Book Resources Ltd.
109 Great Russell Street
London WC1B 3Nd

UNITED STATES and CANADA
Columbia University Press
136 South Broadway
Irvington-on-Hudson
New York 10533

THE LIBRARY
UNIVERSITY OF GUELPH

Preface

A project on budgeting – or on any other subject, for that matter – could not come to fruition without a good deal of prior, innovative, nonincremental 'budgeting' itself. That financial support, as well as some important moral and political support, was forthcoming from several sources over the duration of the project – sources which were willing to take the chance that a study of budgeting in Oslo could yield some payoffs to an international social science community.

The Norwegian Research Council for Science and the Humanities provided the bulk of the financial support, covering generously such items as the hiring of research assistants, the provision for international travel, and salary support. The Institute for Political Science of the University of Oslo provided the chief investigators with time and space to think and write, with competent secretarial assistance, and with additional financial support. The University of Iowa responded generously to a request for release time to collaborate and write during the summer of 1975 by providing one of the authors with an Old Gold Fellowship. Furthermore, the Department of Political Science of the University of Iowa supplied competent secretarial and research assistance over the period. Computer analyses of data were carried out with the help of the computing centers of the University of Oslo and the University of Iowa. Much of that work was done at the Laboratory for Political Research at the University of Iowa.

Institutional support of this sort takes shape only in the form of the individuals whom it brings to the research enterprise; and that list is long. Professors Henry Valen, Ulf Torgerson and Francesco Kjellberg provided intellectual stimulus and practical encouragement (as well as some occasional astute political support) throughout the duration of the project. Tore Hansen participated fully as a co-investigator on the project. His impact is felt throughout this book – not only in Chapter VII, which he co-authored with us, but also in many of the ideas and presentations in the remaining chapters. Frederick Björkan showed extraordinary commitment to the project as a graduate research assistant at the University of Oslo; he conducted many of the interviews and much of the data analysis presented in Chapter VII. Stephen Linder, a graduate research assistant at the University of Iowa, conducted much of the remaining computer analyses with unusual competence and commented perceptively on earlier drafts of this manuscript. Susan C. Cowart provided much of the initial motivation to begin the project, a good deal of competent research assistance for computer analysis during its execution, and unhesitating editorial criticism toward the end. Karen Stewart typed the entire manuscript with a degree of skill and competence which often rendered superfluous our own efforts at proof reading. Finally, this manuscript is undoubtedly better as a result of the efforts of Aaron Wildavsky and Ira Sharkansky, who gave us the benefit of the knowledge and criticism of two of the most important scholars of budgetary processes.

We are obviously indebted to the many officials in the Oslo city government who agreed to respond to general questions which they must often have thought nebulous and to work through a written questionnaire which must have been tedious at best. In writing this, we are reminded of the particular respondent (an agency chief in Oslo) who, upon receiving our request for an interview, tried to persuade us that a collegial, roundtable meeting with several other members of his staff present would be far more preferable and informative and would provide the 'best' set of answers for the interview and questionnaire. As good social scientists, we avoided that, of course, given our desire for single, uncontaminated responses from primary decision-makers. In retrospect, however, it probably would have been one hell of a session – perhaps worth the cost of interview purity; for, it would have come from individuals who showed a remarkable willingness to share with us a lifetime of experiences in doing what they do best – budgeting.

Andrew T. Cowart
Iowa City

Karl Erik Brofoss
Oslo

Contents

I. INTRODUCTION 9
Budgeting: Policy-Making? 10
The Setting: Oslo 16
Plan of the Book 18

II. STUDYING BUDGETARY CHANGE: THEORY AND RESEARCH DESIGN 20
Conceptualizing and Measuring Budgetary Change 21
A Theory of Budgetary Change 25
Research Design 32
Summary 36

III. MULTIPLE ENVIRONMENTS OF BUDGETING: RELEVANT PUBLICS AND PRESSURE GROUPS 37
Clientele Satisfaction and Budgetary Decision 41
Interest Groups and Budgeting 48
Multiple Environments of Budgeting 54

IV. THE POLITICS OF BUDGETING: PARTISAN POLITICS 56
Two Models of Political Effect 59
Party Activism, Political Conflict, and Budgeting 65
Party Support and Budget Success 69
Conclusions: Budgeting and Party Politics 77

V. THE POLITICS OF BUDGETING: ALLIANCE STRUCTURE POLITICS 80
Perceptions of Alliance Elements 81
Alliance Structure Support and Budget Success 88
Conclusions: The Politics of Budgeting 91

VI. ORGANIZING FOR BUDGETING: AGENCY RESOURCES AND BUDGET CHANGE 95
Manipulatable Resources and Budget Change 96

Nonmanipulatable Resources and Budget Change   105
Conclusions   110

VII. STUDYING BUDGETING HISTORICALLY: DECISION RULE ANALYSIS   112
Theoretical Decision Models   114
Model Selection Criteria and Measurement   123
Empirical Results   124
Conclusions, Reservations, and Prospects for Future Research   133

VIII. BUDGETING SYSTEMS: THE POTENTIAL FOR CHANGE   138
The Initiation of Change   140
The Direction of Change   141

NOTES   147

I. Introduction

Policy-making, budgeting, spending, enforcement, program formulation, program evaluation, regulation have all become central elements of what governments do for us or to us in the modern nation state. The increasing importance of governmental life for the lives of individuals is clearly reflected in the renewed interests of scholars in all of these activities in today's public institutions. Indeed, the multiple governmental activities which are now subsumed under the general rubric, 'policy-making', attest both to the richness and diversity of modern governmental affairs and to the inability of scholars to make systematic sense of it all.

This is a study of one important kind of governmental activity – budgeting – in urban Scandinavia. The welfare states of Scandinavia have long held a kind of schizophrenic fascination for Western liberal academicians – admiration for the equity with which components of 'the good life' have been distributed to all citizens, but distaste for the mechanisms of economic control which have been used to generate those egalitarian societies. Such reservations usually take the form of: Where does the money come from? But, that question is wrongly put. Rather, the explanation lies in an answer to the question: Where does the money go to?; for the states of those societies are not the results of historical accidents of massive infusions of wealth but are, rather, the results of conscious choices of people in political and governmental institutions to alter the conditions of man. This study is a snapshot view of that process in one urban locale in Scandinavia – Oslo, Norway.

The central theme, perhaps assumption, is that the existing states or conditions of society at any point in time are affected by the choices of people in public institutions. It is this view of the importance of understanding systematically individual choice which underlies the theory, research design, and analysis strategy of this work. We examine one mode through which individuals in public institutions go about changing societal conditions; more specifically, we focus on changes in financial resource allocation as one way in which policy-makers attempt to alter the policy relevant conditions they face. Our intensive interviews and questionnaire responses from budgeters in Oslo have helped us to understand the environmental, political, economic, bureaucratic, and strategic determinants of those decisions for change. We need to begin, however, by setting out our definitions of policy, generally, and budgeting, specifically, and our conceptualizations of these phenomena as groundwork for our theoretical view of the budgetary process in Chapter II.

Budgeting: Policy-Making?

N subnational governmental units in national governmental unit A each adopt some variation of an income maintenance scheme. Maximum payments, minimum payments, payment methods, eligibility requirements vary across those units. These specific provisions are set in each subnational unit, and supporting funds are budgeted for the program. But, at what point did policy-making occur? Is the policy the content of those provisions or the level of funding for the program? Two decades ago, the answer would have been straightforward: the provisions of the law and of the program and the verbal statements of governmental spokesmen would constitute the policy. Yet, the 'new' policy research of the 1960s and 1970s implies something quite different. These systematic studies of policy are predominantly studies of spending; and it is not at all obvious that the focus of these studies is compatible with conventional, or preferred, usage of the term, 'policy'. More specifically, if we want to claim (and we do) that our study of budgeting in Oslo is a study of policy-making, then we need to specify what it is about the set of decisions on budgets that makes them part of the general class of decisions on policy. We begin by defining public policy.

Public policies are choices, made by people holding authoritative positions in public institutions, which specify how two or more negatively valued future events with perceived non-zero occurrence probabilities are to be processed by governments. We examine the components of that definition, however, for both intuitive plausibility and theoretical utility. First, policies are choices or decisions among alternatives. We hold tenaciously to this component of the definition. We find it difficult, for purposes of explanation, to think of policy-making in other than choice-making terms. Policies do not 'appear' in the absence of individual or collective choice in the same sense that economic development may appear without conscious pursuit of it by individuals, or in the sense that individual political efficacy may develop without an individual purposively striving for it. Rather, policies result when individuals or collectivities make policy decisions.

An objection to the choice-making emphasis of the definition lies in the analysis of what Bachrach and Baratz have called 'nondecisions'. The most significant 'policies' of governments may be those on which there are no explicit decisions. Yet, for purposes of systematic analysis of policy processes, an expanded definition formulated along these lines would lead us to an 'everything-is-related-to-everything' perspective. It would confuse the failure of government to invest resources in changing the infinite number of alternative social states which it might identify with the notion that government favors and promotes the existence of those social states. There is a finite but large number of descriptions of various social states or conditions; but many of these conditions will have developed without ever having appeared on the government's policy-making agenda. Thus, a large number of social states exists as a function of natural processes of economic and social stability and change; these conditions never enter the policy-making agenda of governments; and, since conscious decisions are never made to deal with them or not to deal with them, there are no government policies. These considerations have led us to emphasize the choice-making or decision-making properties of policy and to formulate and implement our research design with some faithfulness to that component of the definition.

The second component of the definition which deserves some scrutiny is the following: Policies are decisions made by individuals 'holding authoritative positions in public institutions'. Certainly we mean to include legislatures, cabinets, bureaucracies, committees, and whatever other structures appear on governmental landscapes. Yet, such a view may be exceptionally formal – and perhaps naive. Specifically, how do we respond to the following entirely plausible observations for various governmental settings: Policies are really set by aristocratic, social notables in Community X, even though they rarely hold formal positions in government; policies are actually determined by the economically active business community, although few participate formally in government; policies are really set by influential political party bosses, although such old-line party pros may not hold formal governmental positions. Any one of these observations may be entirely appropriate for a given set of communities; but there is some danger here in confusing the event with its antecedent causes.

Popular legitimacy has become an asset highly valued by elites in Western nations. Even in the most corrupt of systems, popular legitimacy is sought by having policy decisions, which fall clearly in the public domain, decided by and announced through public institutions. The Chairman of the Board of General Motors in America may ultimately control the outcome of important pollution control decisions, but citizens hear of that policy choice from public officials. Even in such extreme instances, we believe it to be more useful to consider the public official as the policy-maker. We then examine the determinants of that decision, one of which may very well have been the preferences of the Chairman of the Board of General Motors. By retaining a formal, institutional specification of 'policy makers', we hope to maintain some conceptual clarity between the policy choice and the antecedent causes of that choice.

Finally, our definition holds that policies '. . . specify how two or more negatively valued future events with perceived non-zero occurrence probabilities are to be processed by governments'. This last clause distinguishes policy decisions from the multiple other kinds of decisions which are taken in public institutions. We imagine that policy-makers are observing states of nature or conditions in society and that they are making judgments about the consequences (future events) if society is left to its state of nature. In other words, they are engaged in a process of estimating conditional probabilities for negatively valued events:

$$p(R/ x_j, \ldots, x_N).$$

Given observed states of nature $(x_j, \ldots, x_N)$, what is the probability that event R will occur? Policies are instituted to alter that conditional probability. Some examples of this kind of decision-making under certainty, risk, and uncertainty will be helpful.

In this context, decision-making under certainty would mean that the decision-maker knows that p is unity. Such certainty is not as uncommon in policy-making as might be assumed. In a number of different situations, policy-makers behave as if they know that $p = 1.0$; that individuals, left to a purer economic and social state, would behave in certain ways. For example, we know with some certainty that voluntary payment of taxes would yield trivial amounts of revenue, that no (or zero) interest on bank loans would rapidly deplete monetary reserves, and that the American South of two decades ago would have retained segregation without national government interference. Thus, some policy-making contexts are analogous to situations of decision-making under certainty in the sense that nature will produce a given outcome in the absence of a new government policy. If the outcome or event is of sufficient negative value, then policies are instituted to reduce that conditional probability below 1.0, or to lessen the control of nature over the outcome.

Decision-making under risk occurs when conditional probabilities for the occurrence of future events are known to be greater than zero but less than one. It is not known for certain that a given state of nature will produce a given outcome in the absence of government interference, but the probability of such a result is known. This style of decision-making is particularly likely when policy-makers have accumulated experience with existing policies over some extended period of time. Suppose that policy-makers are considering the implementation of a guaranteed minimum income program. Assume that the following three states of nature are the relevant ones for computing the conditional probability that an individual's annual income will not meet minimum subsistence levels in the absence of government involvement: 1) income level of parents; (2) individual's level of education; and (3) individual's race. For uneducated, nonwhite individuals from poor families, we can easily compute the probability that future annual income will be deficient. The probability may be high, but it will be less than unity. Policies are then designed to reduce that probability or, again, to weaken the control of economic and social states of nature on outcomes.

Decision-making under uncertainty describes those policy-making contexts in which the computation of conditional probabilities cannot be so easily accomplished. Policy-makers simply do not know the probabilities that given states of nature will lead to given outcomes. Policy-making under uncertainty is probably most appropriate in situations in which the past frequencies of occurrence of like kinds of events have been insufficient to permit probability estimates. Yet, policies may still result if the event is sufficiently negatively valued by policy-makers. For example, when the American national government instituted freedom of choice plans for public schools, it clearly had no way of knowing the probability that adequate levels of racial integration would result. Particularly, in the South, it 'removed' the policies of state governments and left 'nature' to determine the outcome. Yet it clearly did not know what nature would do.

We find it useful, then, to speak of policy-making as an exercise in which decision-makers attempt to alter the control of nature (nongovernmental conditions and processes) over outcomes. Since few events in society are uniquely determined, we employ the language of conditional probability in which policy-makers are assumed to behave as if they are attempting to change the conditional probability that an event will occur, given certain economic and social states of nature in society. We have purposely avoided terms such as input, conversion, output, allocation, et cetera, for, while these processes are very much a part of the policy-making process, we do not believe that they ought be equated with 'policy' in a definitional sense. Policies are certainly 'values allocated authoritatively', but there are certainly other decisions which do the same. Social welfare case workers allocate valued goods when they decide on client eligibility, but they are hardly making policy. Yet, the question of financial resource allocation and policy-making remains an important one; and, with this conceptual groundwork, we return to that issue: In what sense is budgeting consistent with our definition of policy-making?

While the conceptualization of policy-making as a subset of acts generally called decision-making or choice-making seems reasonable enough, its operational properties prove to be more perplexing. For purposes of systematic research, what are the shared components of the class of policy decisions which allows for comparability across different areas of policy? What, for example, does a policy decision on an income maintenance scheme hold in common with a policy decision on transport service expansion; what do these share with policy decisions on pollution control? The issue is a central one; and, if we cannot solve it, we are left with case studies of particular policy decisions. More specifically, if policies are to be conceived of as reflecting choices for particular alternatives – objects which retain unique qualitative categorizations – then comparability of policy decisions is lost, the range of alternatives becomes unmanageable, the possibilities for systematic data retention become slight, and the natural research focus is toward the case study of specific policy decisions.

The dilemma is similar to that which confronted marketing research on consumer preference behavior some years ago. Systematic assimilation of data on choice proved to be difficult when qualitative categorization of objects was maintained. When a consumer chooses a drinking utensil, he may select a conventional glass, a piece of crystal, a coffee mug, a cup and saucer, a plastic container, and so on. The range of options is considerable and the categorization of choices somewhat clumsy. But if choice is conceptualized as the selection of a bundle of properties rather than as the selection of an object, some of these difficulties diminish. Then, when an individual chooses a drinking utensil, he selects a bundle of attributes; each of these utensils will have a color, a texture, a certain degree of social formality, an ease of handling, and so on.

We may conceive of policy decisions, in much the same fashion, as bundles of attributes; and we represent those attribute levels for a given policy x_j as an ordered m-tuple:

$$x_j = (x_1, \ldots, x_m, x_{i,m+1}, \ldots, x_{i,n})$$

We distinguish between those attributes which are common across many policies $(x_1, \ldots, x_m)$ and those attributes which are unique to particular policies $(x_{i,m+1}, \ldots, x_{i,n})$. The latter are, for purposes of systematic studies of policy, simply disturbance phenomena and must be dealt with through case studies. The former, however, are attributes which many seemingly disparate policies share, although the level of the attribute will vary across those policies.

It is this conceptual view of public policies which allows us to integrate budgeting decisions specifically into the more general class of decisions on policy. Consider, for example, two seemingly disparate policies in the areas of social welfare and transportation. An income maintenance scheme has been adopted, and it is likely that policy-makers considered several properties of alternative schemes before arriving at a final choice. First, staffing is likely to be a key issue. A scheme which could be implemented by drawing upon existing staff and organizational resources may be more attractive than one which requires the establishment of a new bureaucracy. Second, the perceived redistributive impact may be a central issue. For policy-makers concerned with income inequities in society, the scheme with more graduated benefits for low income individuals may be more attractive. Third, the level of funding required to support an income maintenance scheme will be an important consideration. In other words, budgetary allocation is an important attribute of the policy.

A parallel decision on the expansion of local transport facilities may be viewed from a similar perspective. Staffing, redistributive impact, and required budgetary allocations are likely to be key considerations in arriving at a decision, much as they would be in the case of an income maintenance scheme. The distinctions between the two kinds of policies (income maintenance and transport) lie only in (1) the different levels for each attribute which each possesses, and (2) unique properties which may be conceived of as disturbance phenomena. In each case, we may be interested in studying policy change overtime by focusing on changes in staffing level overtime, changes in the redistributive impact of each overtime, and changes in budgetary allocations overtime. It is the latter attribute of policy which we focus on in this book. When we study budgeting, we are studying those attributes of policies which have to do with public financial resource allocation; and we are scoring, for research purposes, administrative units in different policy areas with respect to the level of that attribute which they hold.

Spending is then an obviously important attribute of policy. Few, if any, policies of governments could be implemented and enforced without the use of public funds. We do not, however, claim to be studying other attributes of policies; there are other important dimensions which we shall certainly miss. Yet, the importance of budgeting and spending as one attribute of public policies seems clear. And, it is in this sense that we view studies of budgeting as studies of a subset of the general phenomena we call 'policy-making'.

The Setting: Oslo

The choice of a local Norwegian commune as an appropriate setting for studying these public spending decisions held elements of both intellectual fascination and substantive reservation. One cannot observe the general absence of poverty, the quality of health, the equity in income distribution, the level of prosperity, or the pleasantness of milieu in the cities of Scandinavia without acquiring an interest in how it all came about. Much can be learned about public spending processes by studying those processes in settings where much public spending and government investment occurs – and, not insignificantly, where something about it seems to be working.

Yet, the role of local communal government in the pursuit of the good life in these systems is often ambiguous and is frequently viewed as extraneous – given the extensive arms of the central government in a unitary state. Quite clearly, a study of the spending attributes of policy in local governments has meaning only if local authorities exert meaningful control over the direction of that spending in their jurisdictions.

Hansen and Kjellberg have provided a particularly convincing discussion of how Norwegian local governments maintain a substantial degree of policy and spending autonomy even in the face of extensive regulation by the central government.[2] The central government has some say in most policy areas; but, a detailed consideration of the form of their regulation suggests the extensiveness of opportunities for change at the local level in responding to local conditions. Some areas of municipal activity are, of course, not regulated at all by the central government – support for libraries, orchestras, the arts, and so forth. In other areas such as education and social welfare, the central government provides an extensive list of minimum standards which must be met by local authorities.

Constraints of this kind have not been as serious for public spending in Oslo as might be assumed. First, these are *minimum* standards, and many local communes already exceed them in service provision. Second, the Oslo commune, the largest and most urban in the country, is particularly likely to have exceeded them. The question of meeting such minimum national requirements is now, in most cases, trivial, with more serious policy controversies focusing on how services might be expanded and improved in responding to local conditions and change. In studying budgetary *change* in well-established municipal agencies, we are most likely to pick up responses to changing local conditions over which local policy makers have extensive control – although the 'base' of expenditures may well have been initially stimulated by national law. Thus, the form of inter-governmental relations seems not to inhibit substantially the expansion of service provision or its parallel, the spending of more money for some things, a holding of the line on others.

Oslo provides a particularly appealing setting from other standpoints as well. It bears marked similarity to other cities of its size – about a half million – in Europe and North America. Over this century it has experienced consistent population increases through the middle sixties – a trend which, as in many other cities, reversed itself in the late sixties. The level of industrialization has consistently increased and has brought with it all of the usual problems associated with that process. Population movements to other suburban communes in the late sixties and early seventies have brought with them the problems of declining tax base and an increasingly aged populace typical of other urban areas.

In other economic and social respects, however, Oslo stands apart from other cities of its size. Its location in a country in which roughly three percent of the land is arable has several direct consequences for municipal governmental activities. First, much of the land surface is rock; this, coupled with cold winters of considerable duration, means that the construction of housing units, both single- and multi-family dwellings, is exceedingly costly and time-consuming. Few private enterprises are of sufficient economic size to bear required investments for providing housing on a large scale at moderate costs to consumers. The result has been substantial local governmental involvement in the provision of low-cost public housing. Similarly, short growing seasons and absence of much arable land would create food scarcities and resulting sky-rocketing prices were the municipality not involved in the regulation of consumer prices.

In terms of land area, Oslo is the fifth largest city in the world. The penchant of Norwegians for sport, exercise, and the outdoors, along with the desire to escape the city center, has created demands for use of much of the land as recreation areas; and the municipality is much involved in that service activity. Thus, in all of these policy areas – provision of social services, educational facilities, recreation areas, public housing and others – geographical, social and economic conditions in Oslo serve to heighten the customary demands on local public officials.

The multiplicity of political parties reflects, in many ways, these policy problems which have beset the city in recent times. Each of the seven national political parties finds its counterpart in local politics in Oslo; and the patterns of coalition formation are remarkably similar at national and local levels. Coalitions of the left have included the dominant Labor Party and the smaller Socialist Party and Communist Party, although the Communist Party has not gained a seat on the eighty-five member City Council in recent times. The Conservative Party has dominated bourgeois coalitions, although cooperation with the smaller Liberal, Center, and Christian People's Parties has been required in order to govern.

From an ideological standpoint, debates among party members in the City Council generally parallel this left-right division. Some issues such as parks, recreation, and sports facilities enjoy broad support across these ideological boundaries while others such as social services, public housing, and public transportation divide the parties in more predictable ways. The small Liberal Party has been the swing party to some extent, siding more frequently with the Labor Party on social issues than would have been supposed by its status in the bourgeois group. Others of these smaller parties have tended to become associated with one particular issue.

The overriding concern of the Christian People's Party has to do with the strict regulation of alcohol consumption. The small Center Party, traditionally an agrarian party, has been faced with an eroding base of electoral support in urbanizing Oslo; in recent times, its policy emphasis has shifted to a concern with environmental issues.

Each of these considerations makes Oslo a particularly exciting setting for the study of change in public spending decision processes: (1) a municipal government which, while regulated extensively by the central government, has moved beyond the minimum provisions of national law in responding to rapidly changing local conditions; (2) a set of geographical and demographic conditions which have stimulated governmental activity to a level not seen in many other Western urban areas; and (3) a constellation of political parties which mirror many of the ideological conflicts of their national level counterparts and presumably make their effects felt through representation on a variety of decision-making structures in the Oslo municipal government.

Plan of the Book

We have been especially intrigued with the relationship between changes in financial resource allocations of governments and the environmental, political, structural, administrative, and strategic determinants of change. We have organized this report around just these topics. In the following chapter, we set out the major elements of a theory of budgetary change which guided our research on the budgetary process in Oslo.

Chapter III examines the question of how environmental forces affect changes in the budget prosperity of municipal agencies. Specifically, we examine how (1) policy-makers' perceptions of the satisfactions and dissatisfactions of their relevant clientele and (2) the support they receive from organized interest groups affect their choices and their successes in budgeting. Chapter IV deals with a central issue of both normative and empirical democratic theories – the relevance of political parties for changes in public resource allocations. We consider alternative modes of party support or opposition to budget expansion and assess the net impact of party involvement on budget change at several decision points in the process. In Chapter V, the roles and impacts of different governmental structures are examined; and we focus specifically on the question of support from these various structures and budget change. The analyses in Chapter VI, moving closer to the agency budgeter and his immediate surroundings, focus on the manipulatable and nonmanipulatable resources of individual agencies and their relevance for budgetary change. Chapter VII expands the time period for analysis from a two-year base to a nineteen-year base. Alternative strategies are set out in the form of linear decision rules and their validity assessed with time-series budget data over a nineteen-year period in Oslo. We bring our findings together in Chapter VIII.

II. Studying Budgetary Change: Theory and Research Design

There are no explicit theories of budgetary change. We emphasize 'change' for there are certainly theories of budgeting. Indeed, the concept of incrementalism now holds a pivotal position as an explanation of routine budgetary decision-making comparable to that of party identification in studies of voting behavior or economic development in studies of levels of government spending. We do not quarrel with the view that much in budgeting is deterministic: that programs approved in earlier time periods are not tampered with in later time periods; that some officials and agencies can always expect generous treatment; that many legislatures simply rubber-stamp government-proposed budgets. But it would be extraordinary if many such elements in budgeting were not deterministic. We ask a great deal of governments by requiring them to review funding decisions annually. An individual purchases a private dwelling but reviews with no regularity in later time periods the question of whether he really ought to own the dwelling. Governments, however, are asked to confront this kind of question yearly. That they do not systematically question the validity of these earlier decisions is understandable.

Yet political change is evident in numerous forms in budgeting. Agency officials almost never request the same level of funding from one year to the next. Department level officials prefer and recommend that some units grow and others decline in relative terms in their sectors. Government level officials, responding to a broader set of factors, allow some departments and sectors to grow while others remain stable, or even decline. Legislators focus on elements of government-proposed budgets which are of particular interest to them. Although percentage alterations may be small, legislative changes in relation to prior bureaucratic changes may be rather important. The list could go on, but the significant general point to be made is that the study of budgetary processes, as a sequence of decisions, seems notably sterile in the absence of explicit conceptualizations of change.

Conceptualizing and Measuring Budgetary Change

When we speak of budgetary change, we are ordinarily referring to two general classes of decisions in a sequence of budgetary decisions. First, there are changes in existing conditions or states.[1] Agencies may attempt to alter considerably the levels of funding prevailing in previous time periods. Dramatic increases in appropriations may be requested; those increases may or may not be granted by subsequent reviewers. The focus for this class of decisions is upon change which alters real conditions from one time period to the next. We may observe that kind of change by comparing requested, recommended, or appropriated figures with those appropriated in previous time periods. The focus is on the comparison of preferred states or conditions with existing states or conditions.

A second class of decisions relevant for budgetary change redirects our attention to comparisons of preferred states or conditions among different participants in budgeting. Agency officials prefer one state (as reflected in their budget requests); departmental officials prefer an alternative state (as reflected in their budget recommendations for the agency). We understand an important element of change when we understand or account for the disparities in those preferences. Such disparities occur at other levels as well. The comparison is not between real states and preferred future states but, rather, between two or more disparate future states.

Much of the remainder of this book will be taken up with accounting for these two kinds of change which occur in budgetary decision processes. The point that we are not studying stability, base, or other deterministic elements in budgeting deserves re-emphasis here. The explicit focus is on accounting for and understanding the sources of budgetary change – changes in preferred and actual states in relation to previous time periods and changes in different preferred states for different participants in budgeting during the current time period. We have no doubt that the multiplicity of factors which we examine would be rather irrelevant for understanding the preponderant, stable elements in budgeting at any one point in time. Yet, a focus on budgetary change is another matter indeed.

The institutional arrangements in which budgetary change occurs constitute one of the real constants of governmental organization in the Western world. In Oslo that process is activated when the Chief Municipal Administrator formulates guidelines and forwards those guidelines to department heads and to lower level agency officials. On the basis of these initial guidelines, individual agencies formulate their requests. These requests are reviewed by the department heads, from the standpoint of consistency with both their own views of the sector and the views suggested by guidelines circulated by the Chief Municipal Administrator. Recommendations by department heads are then submitted to the Chief Municipal Administrator, whose task is to produce a coordinated budget for all municipal activities. After consideration of this government-proposed budget by the Council finance committee, the Municipal Council reviews and adopts the budget in final form.

Actual budgetary decisions at each of these four stages in the process – agency request, departmental recommendation for the agency, government-proposed budget for the agency, and Council appropriation for the agency – provide natural bases for operational definitions of budgetary change.[2] We may first define the following quantities:[3]

w_t = agency request in time t
x_t = departmental recommendation for the agency in time t
y_t = Chief Municipal Administrator's recommendation for the agency in time t
z_t = Council appropriation for the agency in time t

Our first conception of budgetary change focuses on comparisons of preferred states with existing conditions. We assume that decision-makers try to alter existing conditions by arriving at decisions which are different from those previously made – in other words, that they compare existing conditions with their preferred states. We operationalize this conception of budgetary change in the following manner:

w_t/z_{t-1} = percentage increase in appropriations requested by the agency
x_t/z_{t-1} = percentage increase in appropriations recommended by the department head for the agency
y_t/z_{t-1} = percentage increase in appropriations proposed by the Chief Municipal Administrator for the agency
z_t/z_{t-1} = percentage increase in appropriations approved by the City Council for the agency

This conception of budgetary change – particularly the fourth quantity – is important for understanding growth in agency budgets over a period of time.

Our second conception of change limits consideration of budget alterations to actions taken during the current year's cycle. Decisions at each of the four stages represent expressions of preferences by each decision-maker. However, we imagine a process which begins, not with considerations of previous appropriations as the baseline, but rather with prior decisions in the current year's budget considerations. We take the initial starting point – the agency request in the current year t – as given; and we focus on subsequent changes in that request as it moves through each phase in the decision process. There are two ways, however, in which that conceptualization of change may become relevant.

First, each reviewer may compare his preferred level of funding for the agency with that recommended at the previous stage of review. Budgeting is, after all, a sequential process. Departmental recommendations for the agency are sent to the Chief Municipal Administrator. The Chief Municipal Administrator's recommendations for the agency are sent to the City Council. If we assume that the focus for decision at one stage is on the recommendation at the previous stage, then comparisons of those two quantities provide appropriate measures of budgetary change. For each agency we refer to these measures of change as level-specific budget change; and we operationalize them in the following manner:

x_t/w_t = departmental recommendation for the agency as a percentage of agency request

y_t/x_t = Chief Municipal Administrator's recommendation for the agency as a percentage of departmental recommendation for the agency

z_t/y_t = City Council's appropriation for the agency as a percentage of the Chief Municipal Administrator's recommendation for the agency

Second, each reviewer may compare his preferred level of funding for the agency with the original agency request (the agency's preferred level of funding). This notion of change similarly focuses on change as reflected in preference disparities between participants in the current year's review process. However, we assume that the important decisional input at each stage is the original agency request – not the recommendation for the agency at the previous stage. This notion of change allows us to trace the cumulative successes of agency budget requests as they move through subsequent decision points:

x_t/w_t = departmental recommendation for the agency as a percentage of agency request

y_t/w_t = Chief Municipal Administrator's recommendation for the agency as a percentage of agency request

z_t/w_t = City Council's appropriation for the agency as a percentage of agency request

We refer to these measures of budget change as cumulative budget change.

We have been fortunate enough to have access to each of these pieces of information (agency request, departmental recommendation, Chief Municipal Administrator's recommendation, and City Council appropriation) for each agency over a period of time. The bulk of this book will be taken up with accounting for budget change in decisions on the 1974 Oslo municipal budget – the time period for which our interview and questionnaire materials are specifically relevant. In Chapter VII, however, we expand the focus by examining patterns of consistency and change over a two-decade period.

The availability of these data on budget change at lower levels in the process is particularly important in European systems. Studies of budgeting in the American setting often focus on budget change as reflected in the difference between government-proposed budgets and actual legislative appropriations. In the American national government, the Office of Management and Budget and the Congress often disagree; sufficient variance persists over the years to make an analysis of those differences meaningful in its own right. The same cannot be said generally of government and legislature in other types of systems in which legislative changes in government-proposed budgets are much subdued. Particularly in systems with some variation on the parliamentary theme of government organization, the 'real action' may be found in the earlier stages of budgetary preparation and review. In these kinds of systems, studies of budgetary change must deal with change at lower levels in the decision process as well as with change at more visible higher levels.

Our dependent variables, then, throughout this study are measures of budgetary change: change as reflected in requested, recommended, and approved increases over prior appropriations; change as reflected in sequential alterations of requests from one reviewing level to the next; and change as reflected in the cumulative alterations of agency requests evident at each subsequent step in the review process. We refer to these conceptualizations of change, respectively, as appropriations increase change, level-specific budget change, and cumulative budget request change. Our specific attempt to deal with budget change rather than with budget base re-opens the question of the volatility of budgeting as a political, resource-allocation process and enhances the theoretical plausibility for hypothesizing effects of a much wider range of societal processes on budgetary decision making.

In the analyses below, we shall often refer to these notions of change in terms of successes and failures, for it is clear in retrospect that our respondents view such changes in just these terms. When a reviewer introduces dramatic cuts into agency budget requests, the result – from an agency perspective – is budget failure. When the Municipal Council returns funds to agency budgets deleted during earlier review stages, the result – from an agency perspective – is budget success. Indeed, agency budgeting is one of the few instances of political conflict and subsequent change in which all participants agree on standards for evaluating outcomes. When an agency budget request, reflecting substantial increases over prior appropriations, sails unmarred through subsequent points of review, the result is budget success; the opposite side of that coin is budget failure.

A Theory of Budgetary Change

We are not able to dissert upon the lamentations of numerous social scientists to the effect that there are no deductive social theories. We must deal, in the sense of Kaplan, with concatenated rather than hierarchical theory – with theory consisting of a set of propositions specifying factors which affect the probability of budget change rather than with theory as a vigorous deductive system in which the component generalizations are logically interrelated.[4] This approach to theory-building has led us to stress analytical foci which would probably be less central had we been dealing with more tightly deductive systems: (1) knowledge of subject matter; (2) patterns of relationships supporting broader interpretations; (3) conceptual frameworks for organizing sets of variables; and (4) interaction of theory and data.

We begin by hypothesizing about the effects of certain factors on budgetary change. That kind of activity would be difficult without some prior knowledge of subject matter – specific knowledge about budgeting in Oslo and more general knowledge about budgeting in other systems. Such knowledge is to the investigator as common sense is to the layman: it is unsystematic; it is piecemeal; it is guesswork. Nonetheless, it is critical as a point of beginning. We know, for example, of specific instances in which certain interest groups had contacted higher level officials on behalf of agency budget requests; and we were aware of some literature on interest groups and public policy formation which suggested that such activity was quite common. These two observations led us to include interest group activity as one element in our theory of budgetary change. The juxtaposition, then, of specific pieces of information which we had about budgeting in Oslo alongside the findings, generalizations, and guesses of prior studies of budgeting provided us with a starting point for assimilating major elements of a theory of budgetary change.

Second, we tried to remain sensitive to the patterns of relationships which – while not necessarily components of the theory – would contribute to theoretical and empirical plausibility. Consider the hypothesis, for example, that political party support contributes to budget success at certain bureaucratic decision points. We might have discovered strong relationships between party support and budget success; but our confidence in the validity of those findings would have been diminished if we could not discover some systematic patterns in the way those effects manifest themselves. We would expect to find considerable variability in the frequency of party contact which itself might be accounted for by the ideological predispositions of parties or the controversial nature of agency programs. We are theorizing, then, not only about the effects of certain factors on budgetary change, but also about patterns of prior relationships as *necessary conditions* – conditions which ought to be documented as a means of enhancing the theoretical and empirical plausibility of our descriptions of budgetary decision-making and budgetary change.

From what we have said thus far, there would be nothing inconsistent with simply accumulating idly element after element in a long list of factors thought to influence budget change. Approaches of this kind, which seek to expand the horizons of earlier studies by taking into account systematically a wide variety of potentially important factors, seem barren without explicit conceptual frameworks. A conceptual framework structures multiple pieces of information about politics. Such structuring takes place as the analyst (1) specifies broader sets of concepts which subsume a number of specific variables within each set, and (2) specifies some broader theoretical link between sets of concepts in ways which allow for natural movement between one set and the next.

The structuring of government and political life constitutes one of the most important means by which elites regulate the floodgates of access, influence, power, and choice. Even in the absence of systematic examination, we could make some important guesses about decisional outcomes simply by examining in detail the organizational charts of government, the formal characteristics of electoral systems, and so on. The multiple ways in which political decision-making processes are organized reveal much about how collectivities of elites viewed the process of policy formation; about how they thought the processes of government and politics ought to be organized.

For our purposes this process of organizing political and governmental relations takes on significance as a process through which elites set probabilities of influence for various economic, social, and political elements in societies. Governments encourage the formation and development of some groups by maintaining frequent contact with those groups; other groups remain more on the periphery. Political parties, in formal terms, have been given even greater opportunities for access by virtue of their formal representation on at least one important governmental institution – legislatures. Bureaucracies and civil servants may be viewed as even more influential, since they bear formal responsibility for a much larger set of specific decisions; indeed, in the case of budgetary decisions, both initiation and review are largely in the formal domain of bureaucracies.

From this perspective we have found the notion of proximity to decision events as a useful one for imposing order on the sets of explanatory concepts we wish to examine. The structuring of governmental and political life imposes substantial structural distance between certain societal elements and the decision-makers responsible for resource allocation decisions at the same time that it bestows proximity on others. We shall consider, in turn, four sets of concepts which we believe may be ordered along such a proximity dimension. The sets of concepts we develop, however, are not mutually exclusive; in the real world, they are closely interrelated in ways which must remain a mystery to us.

The environment of public spending decisions has long been a central focus for analysis by students of administrative systems. By environment, we mean those policy-relevant elements in society which are not formally incorporated into bureaucratic systems and political party systems. Two aspects of the definition deserve re-emphasis. First, environments have too often been conceptualized in global terms rather than in terms specific to individual policy areas. That the level of education of the populace is an important environmental element of administrative systems seems obvious; that the general level of education can account for the variation in choices across administrative units or across policy areas is much less plausible. Thus, we conceptualize environments in differential rather than in global terms. By focusing on policy-relevant elements in environments, we are led to examine the particular environments of different administrative units.

Second, we specify that environmental elements are distinguished from other elements by their formal exclusion from decision-making systems. By definition, these are elements which elites have afforded no formal representation, input, or influence in resource allocation decision-making. It is, of course, implausible to assume that such environmental elements are irrelevant to decision-making processes. Indeed, one of our major purposes in this study has been to understand how individuals and groups who have no formal role in government decision-making continue to make their influence felt at various points in the system.

We believe that there are two principal ways in which those influences might be manifested. First, policy-makers involved in resource allocation decisions may arrive at those decisions by attempting to judge the satisfactions and dissatisfactions of their relevant clienteles – those individuals directly affected by the programs and activities of given administrative units. If such a view of decision-making is appropriate, then environmental effects on public spending decisions would be evident – in spite of the fact that no formal modes of input existed. Yet, the potential for systematic influence is not substantial; for such environmental-decision linkages ultimately depend on the perceptions, judgments, and good will of a large number of administrators and policy-makers.

The second environmental element which we believe has relevance for budgeting is the array of organized interest groups. In the first instance above, we made no presumption of an organized clientele group. Rather, the focus for decision was on an amorphous body of individuals affected by unit programs; and the decisional linkage rested upon the willingness of policy-makers to make judgments about their satisfactions and dissatisfactions. The second form for environmental inputs, in contrast, deals with those individuals in society who have organized for collective action. Such organized pressure groups may demand that governmental agencies do certain things and that higher level reviewing agents, in the case of budgeting, support the programs and activities of agencies in which they have an interest.

The characteristics of these two modes of environmental inputs suggest the tenuousness of environmental-policy linkages. In neither instance have political elites provided for much formal representation on structures of government. In not doing so, they have lessened the probabilities of systematic influence.[5] In this sense, we view these kinds of inputs as the most distant from the standpoint of their linkages to policy formation and resource allocation decisions. The structuring of government and politics has not formally provided mechanisms for their influence; yet, their actual effects on decision and choice remain an empirical question which we expect to deal with in our analysis below.

A second set of concepts, relevant for the explanation of budgetary change, focuses on the pattern of partisan political conflicts. Much research in political science has been directed toward the question of whether policies and spending vary, depending upon which party is in power. We consider that question to be an important one, although there are subtleties obscured when it is formulated in those terms. We want, more generally, to understand whether, how, and why political parties are relevant for budgetary change.

Unlike the elements associated with environmental inputs, however, political parties are not handicapped by formal exclusion from decision-making centers. They are closer to decision events by virtue of their formal representation on several important governmental institutions. Members of political parties constitute exclusively the City Council and the City Cabinet. They serve on various departmental and agency committees. By serving in these and other positions in municipal government, their opportunities for influence on important budgetary decisions are enhanced. Our general question, however, is the extent to which support and conflict among political parties themselves can account for budgetary change.

We believe that the questions raised by dealing with these elements of partisan political life are important both from a normative and an empirical standpoint. Certainly Western normative democratic theory assumes the relevance of political parties – especially in the European setting where more tightly disciplined parties allow majority coalitions to carry out programs and policies which those parties support. In studies of budgeting, however, the importance of parties has too often been assessed by examining legislative votes on government-proposed budgets. As we show in Chapter IV, such assessments will always underestimate the true importance of parties. Rather, a variety of modes of informal influence are available to parties for shaping budgetary outcomes at bureaucratic as well as legislative points of budget formulation and review. Thus, when we speak of the relevance of political party support for budget change, we are referring to both informal and formal opportunities for influence.

It would be natural at this point to develop a third set of concepts which center on the relevance of bureaucracies for budgetary decision-making and budgetary change. Yet, we believe that the important issues are much broader than would be suggested by the politician-bureaucrat dichotomy. The growth in the size of government bureaucracies is only one particular manifestation of the growth in the size and complexity of government structures. The sheer number of government structures in modern Western nations finds no parallel in the forms of government organization even a few decades ago. That the structural expansion of governments has much to do with the expansion of bureaucracies seems evident; but it is more than that. New administrative units are created, but new legislative committees are created as well. Planning units are established within agencies, but permanent political review committees may be established at the same time. Budget officers within administrative units expand their staffs considerably, but so do legislative finance committees.

From the standpoint of explaining important government decisions, the significance of these developments lies in the following: As the growth in the number of government structures proceeds, to what extent does competition between structures in government replace traditional bases of competition (e.g., party competition) as the most important explanation for policy outcomes? Case study accounts of particular policy conflicts provide numerous examples. Municipal planning bodies are established, and their goals and priorities may depart substantially from those held by the governmental units which deal with those substantive policy areas. New structures which deal with, for example, environmental issues may formulate regulations which hamper the efforts of governmental units supporting municipal economic expansion. The significance of these kinds of conflicts is not that they occur between politicians and bureaucrats – for it is rarely possible to sort out participants so neatly. Rather, we may be observing an important stage in policy development in which traditional bases of policy conflict (interest group versus bureaucrat, bureaucrat versus political party, political party versus political party, etc.) are replaced by another kind of conflict – government structure versus government structure. The key to understanding policy outcomes then lies in an understanding of the processes of conflict and compromise between and among important structures in government.

One can imagine a quite different world in the pristine environments of small communities. The organization charts of government are simple ones with few overlapping jurisdictions; politicians and interest groups alike have few difficulties in determining who is responsible for what; and government is not involved in activities complex enough to intimidate the non-governmental participant. With increasing governmental complexity, the arena for policy conflict shifts. The number of structures within government with some say over or input into a particular policy area increases. Conflict increasingly centers on the preference disparities between structures rather than between political parties or between interest groups. And, an understanding of policy outcomes increasingly devolves upon an assessment of the conflicts and compromises among different structures in government.

From the standpoint of our proximity dimension for concept ordering, we have come much closer to the formal center of budget decision-making. We now focus on actual structures in government, many of which hold direct, formal responsibility for decisions on the allocation of community financial resources. Our interest is directed toward the roles of particular structures in budgeting – departments, Council finance committee, City Cabinet, and so on. While party members may indeed be represented on these structures, we assume that it is the particular policy orientation of the structure itself which accounts for budgetary decisions and budgetary change. And, we ask such questions as: How important is support or opposition from the City Cabinet in determining budget change?

Agencies are both our units of analysis and the prime instigators of the phenomenon we wish to study – budgeting. Thus, the fourth set of concepts we develop focuses on characteristics endemic to the agencies themselves. Agencies are, in the sense of our proximity dimension, the closest of all elements to the center of budgetary decision-making. Environmental elements (interest groups, clientele) have no formal opportunities to influence choice and must be content with informal contacts and sporadic access to decision-making centers. Political parties, while their members serve on some institutions in government responsible for budgetary decision-making, may not possess the multiple representations necessary to shape systematically the content of budget decisions at several key points in the process. Specific structures in government – departments, the Chief Municipal Administrator's office, Council finance committee, City Cabinet – may exert substantial influence over outcomes by virtue of their formal responsibility for reviewing initial budget decisions. Yet, none of these elements can match the input provided by the individual agencies themselves. We have been impressed, in examinations of budget figures over time, with just how much of original agency requests remains intact – despite occasional dramatic alterations in percentage terms.

We do not mean to imply that, by developing this fourth set of concepts, we have heretofore excluded agency characteristics. In dealing with environmental elements, for example, we consider the extent to which agency officials attempt to gauge the reactions of relevant clientele to agency programs. But, as an explanation of budget change, it is environment rather than agency which is relevant when such effects are evident. A focus on agency characteristics per se, however, raises different questions. In particular, we ask which factors – associated with purely internal properties of administrataive units – have relevance for budgetary decision-making and budgetary change. Some of these agencies, for example, are large administrative units which devote considerable personnel time and effort to budget preparation, and many have their own planning units whose careful studies may be used to buttress the agency's case for budget expansion at subsequent review levels. Other agencies are not able to benefit from these kinds of structural characteristics. Thus, the fourth set of concepts we develop focuses specifically on those internal characteristics of agencies which might support or retard budget expansion or budget change.

To recapitulate, our theory – as a set of interrelated concepts – conceives of budget change as functions of four kinds of societal processes: (1) the processes by which environmental elements (interest groups and relevant clientele) transmit their demands and/or preferances to decision-makers who bear formal responsibility for budget decisions; (2) the processes through which political party conflict manifests itself in issues of budgeting and funding and the relevance of political party support or opposition for budget change; (3) the processes of conflict and compromise among structures within government and the relevance of support or opposition from various structures for budget change; and (4) the processes associated with internal characteristics of agency decision-making and the relevance of those agency-specific properties for budget change.

These processes are not mutually exclusive; indeed, in the real world they are interrelated at a level of complexity which defies the simplicity with which we set them out here. But, our long-term purpose is to deal with broader explanations of political events, with explanations which link specific resource allocation decisions with important elements of governmental and political life. If any of these explanations prove important or useful, then we will have learned something important about the politics of budgeting, the politics of a decision-making process which often appears markedly deterministic on the surface. The remainder of this book describes how we sought to answer these questions and the results we obtained.

Research Design

Classical research design suggests a paradigm of theory, model, hypotheses, concept measurement, observation, and systematic analysis which often contradicts the real context of research. Only rarely are designs so well specified that the investigator knows where he is going before he is at least part of the way there. In retrospect, we would have it no other way; for knowledge is both dynamic and cumulative, and the directions taken in later efforts ought to be shaped, in part, by what is learned at earlier stages.

We began this study of budgeting in Oslo with a foray into individual agency budgets over a nineteen-year period. In that initial analysis, we pursued the research strategy of formulating a set of linear decision rules and testing those formulations with systematic time series budgetary data; we report the results of that analysis in Chapter VII of this book. For our purposes here, however, one finding in particular stands out: we were never able to account for as much of the variation in agency budget requests as was true for variation in subsequent review decisions of those agency budgets. In other words, we were always more successful in modelling the behavior of agency reviewers than in modelling the behavior of the agencies themselves. Apparently, there was much volatility at earlier stages in the process; and, given the strong impact of requests on review decisions, something in our research design was obviously amiss at that earlier stage. We felt, then, that a compelling case existed for examining decisions, perceptions, and behavior at the agency level as well as the relationship between those factors and other relevant aspects of political life in Oslo.

The documentation of decisions on financial questions is remarkably complete in Oslo. Decisions by budget initiators and reviewers as well as short justifications for actions taken on budgets are matters of public record. Proposals for changes in government-proposed budgets by members of the City Council are made available in those same documents. The relevance of this kind of information for the elements of our theory set out above seems evident – at least on the surface. Yet, it is clear in retrospect that we would not have got very far with an exclusive reliance on such published documents. Reviewers almost always claim that lack of financial resources requires budget cuts; and the effects of political parties will almost always be underestimated with an exclusive focus on their formal behavior in legislative settings. Furthermore, we would have obtained little systematic information on the relationship between environments and budgeting. The natural alternative was the formulation of a more extensive interview and questionnaire scheme. We describe our principal considerations in constructing that document below.

The first and most easily settled question involved who was to be interviewed. Many of these agencies have both an agency chief and a chief financial officer. In most cases, these two individuals have the most say over budget requests. We made an effort to interview both of these officials within each agency. At the conclusion of the interview, we asked if there were any other agency officials who had considerable influence in budget decisions. This turned up only a few additional individuals; in each case those individuals were interviewed. Eighty-three individuals were interviewed; seventy-eight returned a usable follow-up questionnaire by mail.

The questions formulated may be grouped under three kinds of respondent tasks. In some cases, we were interested solely in the respondent's perception of some condition. The assumption is that the way in which he perceives a given condition determines his response to it. Clientele satisfaction is one of the best examples for this class of questions. It is not necessary that the respondent's perception of the condition approximate the true condition in order for meaningful analysis to proceed. Rather, we simply expect that his perception of reality affects choice.

3 – Decisions . . .

A second class of questions cannot be interpreted meaningfully with an exclusive reliance on perception. We imagine that there is some true condition in the real world and that respondents, given their greater familiarity with the condition, are able to give us a better estimate of the condition than could be obtained simply by guessing or by other means. Each respondent was asked, for example, to evaluate the level of support for his agency and its goals provided by each of the seven political parties on scales ranging from 0 to 10. We would not, however, interpret the relationship between those responses and budget change by focusing on the perception linkage. In other words, we would not argue: the greater the perceived support, the greater the budget success at successive levels of review. Rather, the logic of our theory requires interpretation in terms of actual support; and the limitations of this particular analysis are then evaluated in terms of measurement error – the gap between the real condition and the respondent's estimate of it.

A third class of respondent tasks included on the interview/questionnaire schedule may be distinguished from the first two by the relative importance of the measurement error component in the responses. There are certain pieces of information which we need to know about each agency: the number of civil servants employed in the agency, the number of employees who work full time on budget preparation, whether the agency has its own planning unit, and so on. In such cases, we need not be terribly concerned about the measurement error component. Perception is not a relevant linkage concept; the respondent is not asked to estimate some condition on an imperfect instrument. Indeed, we often found that such information could have been obtained from published documents. But, given that systematic interviews were being conducted, it seemed as reliable and more efficient to obtain it from the respondents.

We naturally tried to match the content of the questions on the interview/questionnaire schedule with the four sets of concepts developed above. Yet, as we surveyed the relevant literature on elite attitudes and behavior, we found little assistance in terms of precise wording and phrasing. It soon became clear that, while much excellent literature existed on elite attitudes and behavior, few of those studies contained questions with explicit policy foci. We were faced then with developing new instruments which were, not only policy relevant, but also relevant to one particular dimension of policy – the spending dimension. Thus, the reader will find few familiar measurement instruments in the chapters that follow. We hope that, on occasion, we have broken new ground successfully; that, on balance, our successes outdistance our failures. Yet, we are certain that we have made mistakes; we hope that studies of budgeting which follow will refine and improve the instruments which only approximate imperfectly concepts relevant to budgeting.

It has long been recognized that, in studies of decision-making, the timing of administering interviews and questionnaires is critical. It is not always true, however, that investigators are able to deal with the problem systematically. Not all comparable decisions are taken at the same time for a given set of respondents. In studies of consumer behavior, for example, any given sample would include some respondents who had purchased an item within the last few months and others who had purchased the item as much as five years ago. Studies of budgetary decision-making are analogous to studies of voting behavior in this sense. The timing of decisions is externally determined. Voters cannot choose to cast their ballots six months prior to the election and agency officials cannot receive appropriations at midyear (except in unusual conditions).

It is ordinarily preferable to interview respondents as close as possible to the time of decision. This lowers the probability that various evaluations and judgments have changed between time of recording on the measurement instrument and time of decision. Our purpose was to record information on measurement instruments which would help us to account for decisions on the municipal budget for the fiscal year beginning January 1974. Budget requests by agencies were to be prepared and submitted by late spring of 1973. These requests were to be reviewed and altered by the department heads and the Chief Municipal Administrator during the summer and early fall. Final Council appropriations for each agency were completed during the month of October. We decided that the appropriate time for recording observations was the period between agency request submission and final Council appropriation. Thus, the interviews were carried out and questionnaires were completed during the summer and early fall of 1973.

We were particularly insistent that all information be obtained before final appropriations decisions had been made. Any sequential decision-making process in which the net effect of subsequent decisions during that process is to lessen the level of resources in relation to the level preferred by the initiators cannot fail to generate conflict and some hostility. Since we sought, in terms of the questions formulated, general evaluations of governmental and political life, it seemed preferable to insulate these respondents – as much as possible – from distasteful experiences in one particular year. Thus, the timing of the interviews was such that (1) their own decisions were fresh on their minds; (2) they were unaware of action taken at subsequent levels of review; and (3) their responses were as distant as possible, given these constraints, from decisions taken on the prior 1973 budget. Once the interviews and questionnaires were completed, we simply waited some few weeks until the publication by the government of the final appropriation figures for each agency. That document contains initial request figures by agencies and intermediate reviewer action, as well as final appropriations. We then matched those decisions with each agency chief and financial officer who was interviewed. It is this data-set which serves as the basis for the bulk of analysis which follows.

Summary

In this chapter, we have set out rudiments of our theory of budgetary change, leaving to later substantive chapters a fuller specification of elements, interrelationships, and methods of analysis. We develop three alternative conceptualizations of budgetary change: (1) appropriations increase change; (2) level-specific budget change; and (3) cumulative budget request change. Such changes in budgets are the result of four kinds of broader social and political factors: (1) the policy-relevant environments of administrative units; (2) patterns of support and opposition among political parties; (3) patterns of support and opposition among structures in government; and (4) characteristics endemic to particular governmental units to which those budgets apply. We order these concepts along a proximity dimension which relates their probability of influence to the formal organization of governmental and political life. The extent to which that formal ordering matches real levels of influence is a question we address throughout the book. A research design which relates the responses of decision-makers to actual budgetary decisions helps us answer that question in the following chapters.

III. Multiple Environments of Budgeting: Relevant Publics and Pressure Groups

Social scientists have learned over the last few decades to give some attention to the environments of most social phenomena. The environment in which a young person is socialized is said to affect his or her political attitudes as an adult. The field of comparative public administration has been preoccupied for some time with the question of how environmental and ecological variations affect variations in administrative systems. Recent work on public policy in the American states assesses the impact of a number of environmental conditions on public policy outcomes. Indeed, several bodies of literature are helpful in formulating appropriate conceptualizations and measurements of environmental phenomena.

Three underlying conceptualizations of environment are predominant in the research literature on public institutions: (1) environment as economic and social development; (2) environment as mass publics (clientele) with whom bureaucracies interact; and (3) environment as collections of pressure groups toward whom bureaucracies respond. The first conceptualization is particularly apparent in studies of comparative public administration and comparative public policy. The plea for systematic attention to the environment of administrative systems is most closely associated with students of comparative public administration. Riggs sets forth a series of propositions on bureaucratic development in transitional societies: recruitment and advancement come to be based on achievement; administrative roles come to be highly specialized and differentiated; hierarchical relationships are understood and accepted.[1] These kinds of developments flow from natural processes of economic and social development. Esman, in 'The Politics of Development Administration', equates environmental development with 'changes in system states from peasant and pastoral to industrial organization' and 'the assimilation and institutionalization of modern physical and social technology . . .'.[2] In discussing the ecology of administration, Heady speaks of the wider environment as 'clusters of characteristics, primarily of a social and economic nature . . .'.[3]

37

While the most extensive theoretical treatment of the environment of public institutions as elements of economic and social development is found in this literature on comparative public administration, the most extensive empirical analyses are found in the research literature on comparative public policy of subnational units in North American and Western European countries. Dye, in his *Politics, Economics, and the Public,* measures the policy environments of the American States by the levels of industrialization, urbanization, income, and education.[4] Dye, and others, have then proceeded to assess the relevance of such economic and social conditions versus political conditions as determinants of policy outcomes. Boaden, Alt, Aiken and Depre, and others have replicated that research design in European systems.[5]

For our purposes, this first conceptualization of environment as a society-wide set of economic and social conditions is least useful. We have said that our purpose is to account for the choices of decision-makers in public institutions on questions of resource allocation. First, the variables implied by this conceptualization are not immediately interpretable in decision theoretic terms. To say that 'the higher the level of education in subnational units, the higher the spending per capita' does not mean that decision-makers decide to spend more when they observe higher levels of that environmental property – education. Thus, the interpretative language of 'policy-making' or 'decision-making' or 'budget-making' does not match well with this conceptualization of environmental effects.

A second difficulty is that the properties of environments are conceptualized in global terms rather than in terms of differential elements by policy area. Those properties of environments which may be expected to affect spending across all policy areas – per capita personal income, level of education, revenue constraints, etc. – are selected; those which are specific to specific policy areas are ignored. As a result, these conceptualizations are often counter-intuitive with regard to conventional expectations about environmental effects on policy. For example, increased use of public library facilities – beyond the limits of existing facilities – may be the most important determinant of increased spending for public libraries. Similarly, increased congestion on major motorways may be the most important determinant of increases in transportation expenditures. Yet, these policy-specific environmental effects are lost in conventional global conceptualizations of environments. In addition, the opportunity to account for variations in expenditure allocations is lost, since environmental attributes operate as constants across policy areas.[6]

The second conceptualization of the environment of public institutions focuses on the mass publics or clientele with whom bureaucracies or bureaucrats interact. Katz and Danet have provided what is perhaps the most extensive set of readings on this subject.[7] A large number of studies is compiled which document multiple kinds of effects of client-decision-maker interactions. The assumption of these studies is that the most important properties of bureaucratic environments inhere in the characteristics of mass publics which interact with those bureaucracies; and analysis proceeds with an assessment of the relationships between administrative units and relevant publics. Research interests on official-client relationships typically devolve upon such problems as equity in treatment of individual clients, social determinants of the frequency and effectiveness of interactions, alternative styles of interactions, physical settings of those interactions, etc.

This is a more useful conceptualization of one important component of the environment of budgeting, although we need to move from an individualistic conception of client to a collectivist conception of clientele. 'Annual budgeters' do not provide a service to individual private users in the same sense that 'licensers' provide a service to individual private users. Decisions about budgets for administrative units are more likely to be influenced by cumulative judgments gleaned from interactions with service recipients over an annual period. Thus, we postulate that decision-makers evaluate the degrees of satisfaction and dissatisfaction of their relevant publics and that those evaluations affect budgeting decisions. It is important to emphasize here that there is no assumption of organized pressure group activity. Decision-makers are simply seen as interacting with individual service recipients; and the judgments arising from those interactions affect choice.

The third conceptualization of environment constitutes one of the most pervasive elements in political and social research: the environment as a collection of organized, active pressure groups. Indeed, it often seems that as the size and complexity of society and government increases, organized pressure groups become the only mediators between isolated citizens and large-scale private and public institutions. In understanding the environment-public institution nexus, the group becomes paramount, the individual trivial. Two of the best known works on interest groups in the United States support that general interpretation. In David Truman's *The Governmental Process* and Harmon Zeigler's *Interest Groups in American Society,* cases are discussed at length which support the view that one of the most important environmental elements of public institutions is the extent of pressure group activity, conflict, and contact with those institutions.[8]

Extrapolations, however, to the specific case of budgeting are ambiguous. Certainly Wildavsky has argued that interest groups constitute one of the principal sources of support for agencies and their budget requests in the American national government. Yet, the results of other studies of budgeting, both in the United States and in Norway, cast some doubt on just how systematic and pervasive these effects are. Results from Crecine's computer simulation of municipal budgeting in three American cities suggest that budgeting had become a process largely routinized, internalized, and insulated from these kinds of external pressures.[9] Furthermore, Olsen's study of budgeting in a small Norwegian commune – a study involving extensive interviews with local decision-makers – supports that view of much restrained pressure group activity during budget considerations.[10] Few interest groups were activated during the process of budget preparation and review. Thus, while the conceptualization of the environment of public institutions as collectivities of organized pressure groups seems theoretically useful and intuitively plausible, the evidence for systematic effects is weak – at least with regard to the spending dimension of policy. We shall try to contribute to that body of evidence below.

We begin with a view of the isolated administrator – an extreme case which we believe exists virtually nowhere. Such isolation results when the administrator fails to make judgments about human conditions outside government. His life boundaries are the organization charts of government – boundaries beyond which he neither looks for nor receives stimuli. The environment is, in effect, irrelevant to decision and choice. We cannot imagine such monastic styles in today's public institutions. Most public officials do make judgments about human conditions, think about problems in their relevant policy environments, and receive stimuli about that environment from various external individuals and groups. Yet, it is not obvious that such judgments determine choice. We can well imagine that in bureaucracies largely unresponsive to human needs and environmental demands, such judgments affect only marginally the policy choices of public officials.

Interaction between decision-makers in public institutions and elements in their environments may assume a number of different forms. Two of those forms match the second and third conceptualizations of environments set out above: (1) environments as mass publics or clientele with whom bureaucracies interact; and (2) environments as collections of pressure groups toward whom bureaucracies respond. We examine the perceptions and judgments of agency decision-makers as they relate to (1) judgments about satisfaction of people affected by unit programs; and (2) perceptions about the demands and behavior of organized interest groups. We shall then be able to say something about the consequences of such environmental perceptions and judgments by policy-makers for budgetary actions and budgetary success.

Clientele Satisfaction and Budgetary Decision

An elderly gentleman in Oslo finds walks in the Frogner Park to be a delightful pastime but wishes that more park benches could be provided. A businessman who lives in the suburban community of Nesøya finds daily car travel to the city much easier on the new motorway but would like to see something done about the rush-hour traffic. A mother in the eastern working-class section of the city is pleased that the neighborhood school system is being retained but wishes that the quality of instruction in those smaller schools could be improved for her children. Each of these citizens shares with the others a satisfaction with some aspects of a government service but a dissatisfaction with other aspects of that service. Policy-makers, however imperfectly, attempt to gauge that satisfaction or dissatisfaction. Most policy-makers are likely to form judgments about the degree of satisfaction or dissatisfaction held by their relevant publics – those people directly affected by the activities of their agencies. Indeed, we view these kinds of judgments as one of the more important linkages between environments and public institutions.

We shall use the term, clientele, to refer to those individuals who are directly affected by the programs and activities of a governmental agency. First, few governmental agencies share precisely the same relevant clienteles – although considerable overlap may exist for some. Second, this notion of clientele should be distinguished from the notion of clientele group, which carries the connotation of organized interest group activities. We shall discuss this question of organized pressure groups later on in this chapter; but in this section clientele becomes relevant as a focus for human judgment. While considerable interest group activity may underlie those judgments of clientele satisfaction by policy-makers, it is not central to the analysis. It is quite possible that decision-makers arrive at such judgments in the absence of any interest group's activity whatsoever. Thus, we are interested at this point in the kinds of judgments policy-makers arrive at with regard to the degree of satisfaction held by their relevant publics – those people directly affected by agency programs; for we believe that such judgments have consequences for decisions on budgetary requests and the success of those requests in public institutions.

The dilemmas of measurement are readily apparent in an analysis of this sort. We are two steps removed from a reliable estimate of true clientele satisfactions. First, there will be some slippage between the true degree of satisfaction and the degree of satisfaction perceived by the policy-maker. In addition, there will be slippage between his real judgment and the recording of that judgment on our measurement instruments. The first case need not occupy our attention here, since we assume that it is perception of reality rather than reality itself which affects behavior and choice. The second kind of slippage deserves more careful scrutiny.

When agency officials are asked about the extent of satisfaction/dissatisfaction among their relevant clienteles, that exercise is analogous to one of estimating properties of opinion distributions. Social scientists may attempt to estimate the mean level of political efficacy among different groups of citizens, or to determine whether the distribution of opinion is unimodal or bimodal along a given issue dimension for an electorate. Estimating satisfaction among relevant clienteles is a comparable task for policy-makers – although typically in the absence of systematic information. For our purposes, we may think in terms of formulating questions for policy-makers which ask them to estimate various properties of those distributions. We have dealt with two such distributional properties by asking respondents – circuitously of course – to tell us something about the mean and the form of a distribution of opinion as they see it.

The question in Table 1(a) is strongly suggestive of a mean or central tendency interpretation. The respondent is asked to come to an overall judgment or estimate of satisfaction – from an 'on the whole' or 'on the average' perspective. One agency official who sees different subgroups of his clientele concentrated in different extremes will, nonetheless, come to the same overall judgment as will another official who sees everyone as only moderately satisfied. Similarly, satisfaction for various programs administered by the agency may show considerable variability across programs; but the overall judgment may be the same as for a second agency whose clientele is moderately satisfied with all programs. Thus, this kind of question taps an overall judgment and ignores potential variability in the real distribution of satisfaction/dissatisfaction.

The response pattern in Table 1(b) redirects attention to the form of that distribution. Here the respondent is asked to tell us something of the shape or form of opinion distribution as he sees it. If he indicates that a majority of his relevant clientele is satisfied with the programs and activities of his agency but that a significant minority is dissatisfied, he has, in effect, told us something about his perception of the form of opinion distribution – namely, that it is bimodal and left-skewed. The middle category, on the other hand, suggests that he sees a symmetric bimodal distribution; either end category response indicates a perceived unimodal distribution.

Table 1. Judgments about Relevant Clientele: Marginal Distributions*

(a)
Perceived Level of Satisfaction

Very Dissatisfied									Very Satisfied		
0	1	2	3	4	5	6	7	8	9	10	(N)
0%	0%	2%	2%	6%	15%	18%	28%	16%	13%	2%	(68)

(b)
Perceived 'Shape' of Satisfaction/
Dissatisfaction Distribution

large majority dissatisfied	minority satisfied, majority dissatisfied	half satisfied, half dissatisfied	majority satisfied, minority dissatisfied	large majority satisfied	(N)
0%	7%	24%	40%	29%	(68)

(c)
Action Required to Increase Clientele Satisfaction

Policy Change	Expenditure Increase	Both	(N)
20%	71%	9%	56

* Question wording was as follows: (a) 'If we now look at the people in Oslo who are directly affected by the activities of your agency, how would you evaluate their attitude, generally speaking, toward the activities of your agency? In other words, how satisfied are they?' (0 to 10 scale response). (b) 'How would you characterize that satisfaction (dissatisfaction)?' (Responses were recorded as under (b) above. (c) 'What is the most important thing which the municipality could do in order to increase people's satisfaction with your agency's activities?' (Forced choice response: moderate change in content of policy, substantial change in content of policy, moderate increase in appropriations, substantial increase in appropriations.)

These two questions are not alternative measures of the same underlying phenomenon-perceived clientele satisfaction. Rather, they tap different properties of that phenomenon. Each proposes fundamentally different cognitive decision rules for assimilating or aggregating an individual's perceptions of environmental stimuli. The first suggests that individuals try to make 'on the average' judgments about those conditions. The second suggests that individuals' attention is drawn to significant pockets or concentrations of satisfaction or dissatisfaction. The marginal distributions for responses to these two questions demonstrate sufficient variability to allow us to move on to a more important question – the consequences of such judgments for public spending decisions.

Before doing so, however, one question needs clearing up about the conditions under which clientele satisfaction/dissatisfaction produces significant budget effects. It is not necessarily true that dissatisfaction among relevant publics can be traced directly to problems of inadequate program funding. Public dissatisfaction with governments may be closely tied to the content and administration of program and policy; it may have little – indeed, nothing – to do with budgeting and spending. In such cases, widespread dissatisfaction among relevant publics would be expected to produce few – if any – ramifications for budgeting. Thus, we need to address this question from the standpoint of necessary conditions for any subsequent meaningful analysis of clientele effects: Do agency officials view whatever dissatisfaction that does exist as amenable to change through increased spending? That question seems well answered by the entries in Table 1(c). The marginal distributions themselves are revealing on this point: nearly three-quarters of these officials agree that the most effective action to improve clientele satisfaction is an expenditure increase. Here the message is clear and leads us to anticipate substantial effects of judgments about clientele satisfaction on budgetary decisions.

We wish to deal, then, with two conceptions of how individuals in

Table 2. Relationships between Perceived Level of Clientele Satisfaction and Budget Change
(Pearson product-moment correlation coefficients)

Level-Specific Budget Change	
dept rec/agen req	.175
CMA rec/dept rec	.237*
Coun app/CMA rec	.211*
Cumulative Budget Change	
dept rec/agen req	.175
CMA rec/agen req	.245*
Coun rec/agen req	.297*
Appropriations Increase Budget Change	
agen req/prior app	-.168
dept rec/prior app	-.152
CMA rec/prior app	-.106
Coun app/prior app	-.081

* Statistically significant at .05 level; n = 68.

government institutions assimilate or summarize information about their environments – in this case, the satisfaction of their relevant clienteles. One suggests that individuals arrive at 'on the average', 'on the whole', or 'mean' kinds of judgments. The other suggests that attention is drawn to concentrations, shapes, or forms of opinion distribution. The relationships between the former kind of judgment and budgetary decisions and budgetary success are shown in Table 2, and those relationships vary between weakly significant and insignificant levels. For level-specific budget change and cumulative budget change, there is some evidence that high levels of clientele satisfaction strengthen the agency's case for obtaining requested increases. Yet, these relationships are not of sufficient magnitude to account very well for variations in budget success. The problem is presumably not one of variance since there is considerable variability across individuals (Table 1). Rather, such 'central tendency' kinds of judgments seem not to affect appreciably the magnitude of requests or the success of those requests at subsequent reviewing levels.

The second conception of how individuals assimilate stimuli about environments directs attention toward the shape or form of opinion distributions. The underlying response model is quite different: it suggests that individuals respond to and make judgments about concentrations of opinion – symmetry, modality, etc. The effects of those kinds of judgments are shown in Figure 1. The means for each alternative measure of budget success are shown for each level by clientele satisfaction. Line A in each graph plots those means for agencies in which a large majority of clientele is seen to be satisfied (a perceived unimodal, left-skewed distribution of satisfaction opinion). Line B represents those agencies for which a majority is viewed as satisfied but a significant minority is apparently dissatisfied (bimodal, left-skewed). The means for line C in each of the graphs are based on those agencies in which at least half or more of relevant clientele is viewed as dissatisfied (unimodal or bimodal, right-skewed).

These entries deserve considerable scrutiny for they are suggestive of the subtleties – indeed, contradictions – inherent in the process of budget formulation and review. For level-specific success and cumulative success, the most successful agencies are those for which a large majority of clientele is seen to be satisfied (line A). When a significant minority is seen to be dissatisfied, however, budget success at these reviewing levels diminishes somewhat (line B). Those agencies for which half or more of their relevant clienteles are perceived to be dissatisfied are apparently the least successful of the three groups (line C). If attention is restricted solely to these first two graphs in Figure 1, conclusions are somewhat unsettling, for they suggest that reviewers

Figure 1

Perceived 'Shape' of Clientele Satisfaction Distribution and Budget Change

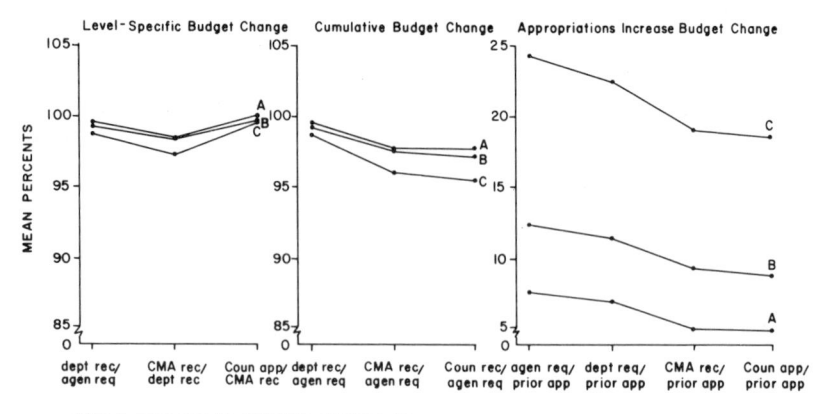

KEY: A. large majority of clientele satisfied; n=20
   B. majority of clientele satisfied, minority dissatisfied; n=27
   C. half or more of clientele dissatisfied; n=21

are least sensitive to the needs of those agencies where clientele dissatisfaction is presumably greatest.

Yet the third graph in Figure 1 clarifies considerably the patterns found in the first two. Indeed, we would arrive at precisely opposing conclusions about the effects of clientele satisfaction on budget change, depending upon which of the three conceptions of budget change (level-specific or cumulative change versus appropriations increase change) was chosen. An important key to disentangling these seeming contradictions, however, lies in an examination of the means for agency acquisitiveness (agency request as a percentage of prior appropriations) in the third graphical display. First, the effects of such judgments about clientele satisfaction on agency acquisitiveness are dramatic. When the perception is that a large majority of clientele is satisfied with agency programs and activities, the requested increase is, on the average, a mere 7.5 percent (line A). When a significant minority is seen to be dissatisfied, however, that level of acquisitiveness jumps to over 12 percent. Finally, in those instances in which half or more of the agency's relevant clientele is judged to be dissatisfied with current agency programs and activities, requested increases exceeding 24 percent are customarily sought – in a presumed effort to lessen that dissatisfaction through increased spending. Furthermore, these differences are maintained throughout successive levels of review. Thus, the outcome of budget considerations – as measured by the percentage increase over last year's appropriations actually granted by the Council – is quite reflective of these initial judgments about satisfaction of agency clientele: the more extensive the perceived dissatisfaction, the greater the increase in appropriations.

With these patterns in mind, we may now discuss the question of why these apparent contradictions occur when alternative measures of budget change are used. Such patterns are the probable result of the following rather common decision scenario: Agency officials are sensitive to the satisfactions and dissatisfactions of people who are directly affected by their programs. When dissatisfaction is perceived to be considerable, dramatic increases in appropriations are requested by those lower level officials. Yet budget problems for higher level officials are simply of a different sort – e.g., producing balanced budgets, operating within certain guidelines and revenue constraints. Reviewing agents apparently view with a natural suspicion excessive attempts at budget expansion – even when such expansion is based upon the best of intentions. One consequence of this is that those 'clientele-responsive' budget requests are treated more severely (as indicated by the differences in means for the first two graphs or the differences in slopes for the third). Yet, the severity of that treatment is not of sufficient magnitude to diminish the markedly higher overall success rates of the expansive agencies. The end result is that the sharpest increases in appropriations from one year to the next continue to go to those agencies which must deal with a substantial body of dissatisfied clientele.

The nature of the dilemma faced by budget reviewers is clear in such instances: their behavior – as measured by action taken on budget requests – *looks as if* they are penalizing those agencies where clientele dissatisfaction is greatest. And, we can imagine that much hostility is generated during budget considerations from just this kind of observation. Certainly deletions from budget requests are most severe in those cases. Yet we need to probe beyond that initial observation to the point of request formulation. Lower level officials are quite responsive to judgments about clientele dissatisfaction. Such judgments lead to drastically expanded request figures which, in turn, lead to more excessive cuts by reviewers. Two countervailing effects are evident here. Reviewers treat expansive budget requests more severely – even when that effort at expansion was precipitated by judgments about clientele dissatisfaction. Yet, reviewers continue to allow those agencies to experience higher growth rates in terms of appropriations increases. While in terms of specific action on request, the budget system appears markedly unresponsive to needs and dissatisfactions, it is in fact quite responsive in terms of overall outcomes or actual growth rates in appropriations.

Interest Groups and Budgeting

The demands, preferences, and priority judgments of organized interest groups have always been seen as important foci of governmental decisions in healthy pluralist democracies. The view of interest groups as vehicles for assimilating the preferences of their members and for pressing government officials for actions consistent with those preferences has much currency in Western democratic theory. Yet, the role of interest groups in questions of resource allocation remains a subject of some confusion. Indeed, the implication of some recent studies of budgeting is that interest group effects are negligible.[11] We wish to address this question by first conceiving of interest groups as a second important element in the environment of public institutions – an element which may become an additional focus for human judgment about environmental conditions. We wish to know something about the elements of environments toward which the attention of public officials is drawn. In the first instance, we examined the utility of a clientele focus – an amorphous body of individuals who are directly affected by the programs and policies of a governmental unit. The second element of the environments of public institutions which we wish to develop here departs from the first. We hypothesize that the focus of attention of decision-makers is on the organized group – rather than on the amorphous bodies of clientele – and we view this kind of focus as a second mechanism by which decision-makers read and evaluate their relevant environments.

It is useful to distinguish between two alternative modes of effects which might be observed. First, interest groups may have considerable input into the formulation of budget requests by agency officials. Program expansions may be proposed in ways and at levels consistent with the preferences of relevant groups. Once those decisions have been made, however, interest groups may become important in a second respect. Interest group activity may become characterized by supportive efforts at subsequent levels of budget review. In other words, the focus of activity shifts to the points of budgetary review, and the effort becomes one of insuring that proposed agency expansions are not deleted by those reviewers.

In either event it is important to examine initially some necessary conditions if effects of this kind are to be felt. We need to know something about the nature and extensiveness of interest group contact with governmental agencies and their reviewing agents. If it is true that interest group contact with government agencies is only sporadic and infrequently related to questions of program funding, then our statements of overall effects need to be muted. Similarly, overall assessments of interest group effects at subsequent levels of review ought to be much restrained if such contact with higher level reviewing agents occurs only rarely. Thus, two kinds of questions are relevant here: how pervasive are the contacts with regard to budgetary questions; and, what are the effects of such contacts?

The entries in Table 3 indicate the frequency with which various types of interest organizations interact with municipal decision-makers in Oslo. Respondents were asked, in free-answer format, to list the organizations with which they had contact regarding agency activities. Labour union contacts typically involve such issues as the improvement of employee working conditions and movement of employees into better pay categories. Among professional organizations, the Norwegian Doctors Association is particularly active on questions of organization of service arrangements in municipal hospitals, methods of payment of doctors, etc. Various local neighborhood organizations have become particularly active in Oslo in recent years – contacting the municipality on issues of neighborhood beautification, street closings, and park maintenance with some persistency. The other political organizations are not political party organizations but rather youth movements and party youth groups.

The activities of religious organizations are instructive on how interest groups may come to have a direct bearing on municipal finances. Religious organizations have been quite involved in establishing homes for the disabled, for drug addicts, for alcoholics, and for individuals who no longer require intensive psychiatric care. It is not uncommon for these organizations to set up such establishments and, subsequently, to ask the municipality to provide funds for maintaining them. The argument, of course, becomes compelling for providing such funds, since the initial capital investment would have been provided free to the municipality (i.e., by the interest group itself). Other kinds of interest groups have used this same strategy. The establishment and maintenance of the municipal school for seamen and of local private hospitals are good examples. The inputs of cultural and sports organizations are more directly linked to large capital investments. The municipality is asked, with some frequency, to provide concert houses, exhibition halls, neighborhood sports facilities, support funding for theatrical activities, and so forth. These case observations lead us to expect some systematic effect of interest group activity on municipal budgeting decisions.

The marginal distributions in Table 4 reveal something of the properties of interest group contact at the agency level. Each respondent was asked during the interview to indicate the organizations with which he had some contact (Table 3). That question was followed by three closed-ended questions directed toward several characteristics of that contact: (1) whether it was continuous or sporadic; (2) whether it usually focused on the carrying out of existing activities or the proposing of new activities for the agency; and (3) whether it usually involved questions of funding and expenditures or questions of a more substantive or policy nature. Most of these officials apparently see their contact with various interest groups as continuous rather than sporadic. The resulting input apparently centers on problems associated with the carrying out of existing programs. Fewer than one-fourth of these officials indicate that the alternative innovative kind of input – the proposing of new activities – is very common.

Table 3. Distribution of Types of Budgetary Active Interest Groups

Interest Group Type	Percent of All Mentions
labour unions	17.1%
professional organizations	14.7
local neighborhood organizations	7.7
other political organizations	3.8
religious organizations	7.0
cultural/sports organizations	22.6
humanitarian organizations	13.2
other	13.9
Total	100.0%
(N)	(128)

The third set of entries in Table 4 is most relevant for the study of resource allocation, and here the message is reasonably clear: while interest group contacts with agency officials may be quite frequent indeed, the content of those interactions does not reflect questions about the adequacy of program funding. Rather, the content of such input simply involves more substantive kinds of questions associated with the content of existing policies and programs. While interest groups do not appear to show every creative kind of inputs (a focus on existing activities), they do appear 'live and well' from the standpoint of frequency of activity (a pattern of continuous contact); yet their effects on budgetary decision-making at the agency level are likely to be slight.

The predominant kinds of inputs simply do not involve questions of program funding and expenditure.

We may pursue this notion of establishing a set of initial conditions before assessing effects for reviewer decisions as well. Once agency budget requests have been proposed, it is likely that interest groups may be activated during the review process. One form which that activism may take is direct contact with appropriate reviewing agents and other influentials. In contacting these budgetary influentials, organized groups presumably press the agency's case and attempt to insure that requested funds for programs – in which their interest lies – are not deleted during budget considerations.

Table 4. Relationships between Estimate of Percent of Budget Bound by National Law and Budget Change
(Pearson Product-Moment Correlation Coefficients)

Level-Specific Budget Change	
dept rec/agen req	-.101
CMA rec/dept rec	.113
Coun app/CMA rec	-.073
Cumulative Budget Change	
dept rec/agen req	-.101
CMA rec/agen req	.028
Coun app/agen req	-.012
Appropriations Increase Budget Change	
agen req/prior app	-.217
dept rec/prior app	-.226
CMA rec/prior app	-.206
Coun app/prior app	-.212

Statistically significant at .05 level; n = 58.

The entries in Table 5 refer to the question of frequency of such contacts at various levels. These agency officials were asked to indicate how frequently interest organizations contacted specific municipal organs on their behalf concerning budget questions. While a good deal of variability across potential points of contact is evident in Table 5, the overall view is one of considerable interest group activism. Indeed, over one-half of these officials indicate that organized interest groups contact the various political party groups and the department head in support of agency budget efforts. It is interesting to note that the most influential of decision-makers – the Chief Municipal Administrator – is apparently the least accessible – a point to which we return in Chapter V.

Our examination of these initial conditions for interest group effects leads to several summary statements about interest groups in municipal politics in Oslo. Such groups are indeed active, both in terms of continuous direct contact with municipal agencies and in terms of support for those agencies' budgets during the review process. In the former case, however, an important qualifier is that such contact rarely focuses on questions of budgeting and spending. Such patterns suggest the following with regard to actual budget effects: The inputs of organized interest groups have negligible effects on budgetary requests for lower level administrative units; interest group support for those agency budget requests at subsequent reviewing levels, however, is likely to be an important determinant of budget success for those agencies.

Table 5. Focus of Interest Group Contact*

	Percent of agency officials indicating, at each level:		
	frequent contact	infrequent contact	(N)
Party Groups	56.9%	43.2%	(51)
Department Head	51.0	49.0	(51)
Layman Political Committees	43.1	56.8	(51)
Cabinet	35.3	64.7	(51)
Mayor	31.3	68.7	(51)
Council	21.6	78.4	(51)
Chief Municipal Administrator	18.0	82.0	(50)

* Question wording (forced choice): Do these organizations which you have named ever contact other municipal organs or individuals on your behalf when your agency budget is under consideration? (often, occasional, seldom, never).

In answering this kind of question, it is useful to distinguish those agencies which operate in environments characterized by considerable interest group activism from those which operate in more placid environments. We specify an active interest group environment by observing the following response patterns: an agency official indicates that relevant interest groups *frequently* contact *two or more* access points (listed in Table 5) on his behalf during budget considerations. These responses were originally obtained along a four-point scale for each access point. Respondents indicated whether relevant interest groups contacted each specified access point 'often', 'occasionally', 'seldom', or 'never'. Frequent contact is specified by the former two responses; infrequent contact by the latter two. Thus, if a respondent indicates that interest groups contact at least two access points often or occasionally, his environment is defined as one of high interest group activism. If these response conditions are not met, then the environment is one of low interest group activism.

The graphical displays in Figure 2 show the mean level of budget success for the two groups of agency officials – those which operate in a highly active interest group environment (line A) and those which do not (line B). These formulations allow us to trace the budget success of each group at each stage in the process of budgetary review. While the differences are not substantial in the case of level-specific success, they are quite consistent at each level of review. For agencies with considerable interest group support, the department head typically grants a larger percentage of the original agency request, the Chief Municipal Administrator typically grants a larger percentage of the departmental request for the agency, and the Council responds similarly to the Chief Municipal Administrator's recommendation for the agency. Indeed, the cumulative or net effect of interest group activism is about three percent. In other words, those agencies with considerable interest group support can expect to receive, on the average, about three percent more of their original budget request than would be true for those without such support.

Figure 2

Interest Group Contact on Agency Behalf and Budget Change

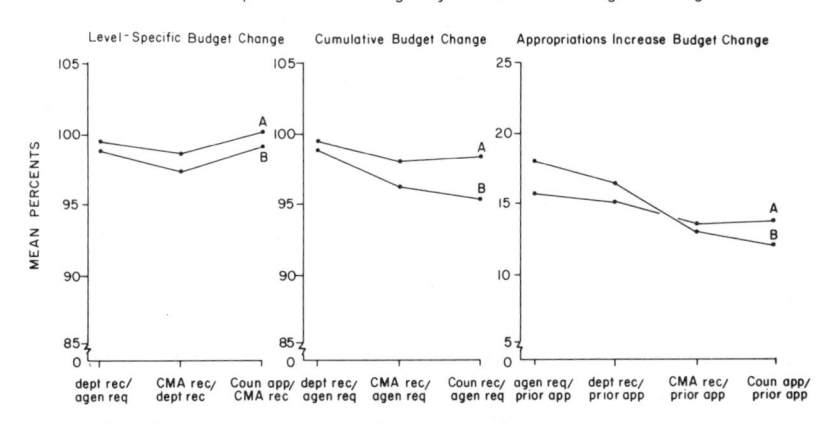

KEY: A. Interest group contact at multiple access points on agency behalf; n=32
B. Interest group contact at single or no access point on agency behalf; n=51

The third graph in Figure 2 provides more dramatic evidence with regard to interest group effects on budget expansion. First, from Table 5 we drew the inference that the inputs from organized groups would have negligible stimulative effects on agency budget requests – since those inputs rarely concern questions of funding. That view is borne out by an examination of the mean agency acquisitiveness for the two groups. Indeed, those without much interest group support are somewhat more acquisitive than are those who benefit from such support. Yet, it is clear what happens to the two groups as those requests move through the review process. Those agencies operating in an environment of substantial organized group activism and support lose, in a net sense, only about two percent of their requested increases. The losses for the alternative group are, on the average, three times as great.

Not only are the net differences consistent with that interpretation but the trends of the two lines are consistent as well. At every point, the slopes are greater for the non-supported agencies than for the supported agencies. Furthermore, this is one of the few instances in which an independent variable serves to mute the effects of initial agency acquisitiveness. Ordinarily, lines of this sort (showing mean levels of agency acquisitiveness and success by categories of an independent variable) do not cross; the acquisitive budgeter holds the advantage as measured by final appropriations increases. In this case, however, interventions by organized groups on behalf of agency budget requests at subsequent reviewing levels can be crucial in securing those requested increases.

Multiple Environments of Budgeting

In this chapter we have tried to move beyond the organization charts of governmental units to an assessment of the impact of the wider environment on public spending decisions. We have not dealt, however, with the customary environmental variables of policy research – the level of industrialization, per capita personal income, the level of education, etc. Rather, we develop the view that the appropriate environmental arena is a variable itself; no two governmental units will share precisely the same environment. As a result, our research strategy has been to ask public officials about some of the properties of their relevant environments.

We have set forth two alternative mechanisms by which the attributes of relevant environments may affect resource allocation decisions: (1) Agency officials attempt to gauge the satisfactions and dissatisfactions of their relevant clientele; those assessments enter the decision calculus for budget request formulation and serve to strengthen the agency's case when those requests are subsequently reviewed. (2) Agency officials attempt to read the preferences and demands of organized interest groups. Those readings are reflected in budget request decisions; furthermore, organized interest group support at subsequent reviewing levels contributes measurably to agency budget success.

We have not found that environmental effects are as pervasive at each level as these sets of propositions would suggest. Rather, different properties of environments affect decisions at different points in the process of budget formulation and review. The efforts of lower level officials to alleviate substantial pockets of clientele dissatisfaction have primarily a stimulative effect on budget expansion. Agency budget acquisitiveness is simply much greater for instances in which considerable clientele dissatisfaction exists. The effects of such factors at subsequent levels of review, however, are negligible. Agency officials who can point to these kinds of conditions are apparently no more successful than are other officials in steering those requests through successive levels of review. In terms of final appropriation increases, however, these officials are indeed more successful – a result, however, of their initial heightened acquisitiveness to begin with.

The significance of the second environmental element – the preferences and demands of organized interest groups – is simply of a different sort. The consequences are negligible at the stage of agency budget formulation. The nature of pressure group input for governmental agencies rarely has much to do with questions of funding. The chief consequences of organized interest group activity are found during the period of budget review by higher level officials rather than during the period of budget formulation by lower level officials. The budgets of those agencies which cannot depend upon relevant interest groups to intercede on their behalf during the review process suffer dramatic cuts. In contrast, those agencies which operate in a more active interest group environment may expect to see their budgets cut by trivial or insignificant amounts.

IV. The Politics of Budgeting: Partisan Politics

It is extraordinary to raise the question of whether politics matters for important government decisions; of course it does. Politicians establish and expand the institutions in which government decisions are made. They make countless decisions themselves as members of elected legislatures and cabinets. Even when responsibility is delegated to public servants, politicians have the final say on issues ranging from the rules which prescribe how those same public servants will be selected to the guidelines which prescribe the limits of acceptable decision across a host of policy areas. Administrators themselves have come to play political games at a level of competence not realized in earlier decades of political research. The appropriate question is not whether politics matters but rather how and why it matters. The appropriate theoretical questions center upon the development of hypotheses and explanatory statements which may illuminate those linkages for which, as yet, much muddy water remains. The concomitant problem for research on politics is the formulation and discovery of methods which may be used to monitor such effects of politics on government decision.

It was not many decades ago that to speak of politics was to speak of party. The study of politics was, in one form or another, related to the study of political parties. The assumption was that the institution, not the act, defined the areana of politics. The traditional distinction in public administration between politics and administration reflected such an assumption. Political activity and controversy occurred in political institutions – party organizations, legislatures, cabinets – and administrative activity – budget formulation, program implementation, control – occurred in bureaucratic institutions. One of the tangible contributions of the behavioral era in political research has been the recognition that political activity occurs in all institutions. More significantly, we have come to accept an 'activity' rather than an 'institutional' definition of politics. Politics takes place when individuals compete for scarce resources. Thus, researchers are able to observe and to study political activity in a variety of institutional settings – bureaucracies as well as legislatures, hospitals as well as party organizations, schools as well as cabinet committees.

We view this expansion in the focus for research on politics as a healthy development. Particularly for the study of public budgeting decisions, it allows us to examine the budgetary consequences of political activity in the several government institutions which participate formally and informally in the budgetary process. From this perspective we shall be particularly concerned with the nature of political conflict in government. A cursory examination of the development of government in the modern world could not fail to document the growth in the sheer number of government structures. In contrast to earlier times, the multiple number of government structures which participate in important government decisions is evident. For budgeting in Oslo, for example, agency officials formulate their budget requests; department heads pare down those requests, but layman political committees have significant input at that point; the Chief Municipal Administrator revises those departmental recommendations, but the Mayor and the City Cabinet are likely to make their wishes known during such a review. The Council Finance Committee works over that government-proposed budget – changing some items itself and leaving other changes to the whole Council. Thus, at least seven government structures (apart from the agency itself) may have significant input into budgeting decisions.

But the growth in the number of such participating structures raises important questions about the nature of political conflict in government. In particular, these developments cannot fail to have consequences for party government. The centering of important policy controversies on the disparities in preferences among different structures provides a backdrop for the demise of party in government. Political parties may continue to take distinguishable stands on policy issues; but the outcomes are determined through bargaining between the Chief Municipal Administrator and the Council Finance Committee, not through bargaining between the Labor and Conservative Parties. The key to understanding the politics of budgeting may lie, then, in an examination of the conflicts, compromises, and alliances among structures in government themselves. Thus, the question we pose in this chapter and in the next is the following: Are policy controversies and compromises in government the result of conflict among parties, as might be deduced from the responsible parties model, or the result of conflict among structures, as recent developments in the growth of government and much recent political research would seem to suggest?

These two themes have been central ones in studies of the politics of policy formation in recent times. The modern intellectual roots of issues surrounding the notion of political party and government policy may be traced back to the works of V.O. Key, Jr. and the American Political Science Association's Committee on Political Parties in the early 1950s. The Committee called for more responsible American political parties – responsible in the sense of providing meaningful, programmatic alternatives to American electorates; the assumption was, of course, that such programs could be implemented once the party gained power.[1] In a parallel vein, Key argued that heightened competition between the two parties would lead to new and different governmental policies, as parties sought to expand their pools of supporters among electorates.[2]

These issues were important ones; they struck at the heart of the question whether political man can ever organize governmental and political life in such a way as to reverse more natural processes of economic and social order. American scholars obviously believed it to be possible, for they pointed to the successes of party government in the parliamentary systems of Western Europe. Indeed, the British system of cabinet government remained the ideal. Although current day evidence remains paltry, such assumptions were not unfounded. The research literature on subnational policy outcomes in America picked up on this theme and soon discovered that it matters little for public spending whether Democrats or Republicans control state governments.[3] The method spread; and students of subnational policy outcomes in Britain subsequently found the reverse.[4] It apparently matters somewhat whether Labourites or Conservatives hold borough council majorities.

The second theme – the importance of conflict between structures in government – seems much less explicit but fully as pervasive in the research literature on policy formation. Wildavsky's classic, *The Politics of the Budgetary Process,* provides the clearest in depth discussion of how conflicts and compromises among structures in government affect government policy.[5] The multiple strategies which lower level, intermediate, and higher level decision-makers follow in dealing with each other and with legislative committees attest to the centrality of this kind of conflict in policy making. We develop below some skeletal elements of two models of political effects on budgeting which are drawn from these initial thoughts on the relative importance of governmental structures and political parties for budgeting; and we assess in some detail the explanatory power of each in this chapter and in the next.

Two Models of Political Effect

We refer to the first model of political effects on budgeting as the party programmatic model. Its elements depend upon some deductions which can be made from the responsible parties model in democratic theory. The responsible parties model, as its name implies, affords a central role to political parties which take distinguishable stands on important issues. Its counterpart in the case of budgetary politics would find the parties dividing in predictable ways on questions of resource allocation for various programs and governmental units. We might expect, for example, that parties on the left support the expansion of agencies which carry out social welfare activities while parties on the right oppose such expansion. Similarly, parties on the right may support budget expansion efforts of those agencies involved in social control in the face of opposition by parties on the left. Furthermore, if this party programmatic model is the more appropriate one for understanding the importance of politics for budgeting, then support from political parties should have substantial consequences for budget success.

For the party programmatic model, political parties are presumed to reward those governmental agencies carrying out programs which those parties strongly support. Whether linked to conceptions of constituency support or consistency with party ideology or issue positions, party members in the legislature or in other positions of influence are presumed to make judgments and subsequently engage in efforts to support expansions of programs favored by that political party. The distinctive property of the party programmatic model of budgetary support is that the support accruing to an agency from a given party is, in the extreme, solely a function of the consistency of the agency's activities with party programs, ideology, or issue positions.

As we have suggested above, however, a major thrust of recent research in political science is that politics occurs in all institutions – not just in political parties and legislatures. This view is reflected particularly in the research literature on the determinants of budgeting decisions and expenditure levels. Much is made of the political conflicts and compromises among influential administrators. The argument is that the successful agencies are those which have been able to build up strong bases of support at several key points in the governmental structure. We may posit, then, a second model which explains how politics is important for budgeting; and we refer to it as the alliance structure model.

This second conception of political influence on budgetary decisions is both less purist and less partisan. It conceives of budgetary success for a given agency, less in terms of the consistency of agency activities with party programs, and more in terms of the alliances which the agency has been able to establish over the years – alliances which, though often partisan, may cross-cut different political parties in various ways and, indeed, may not center upon party at all. It suggests that those agencies which are successful in expanding their activities are those which have built up bases of support (alliance structures) at several critical points in the budgetary process. In other words, it suggests that any of several participants or organs may be quite influential during the budgetary considerations preceding the final appropriation stage, and that those agencies which have built up strong alliances or bases of support at these critical junctures may be the more successful in steering their requests through the process. Several works on budgetary decision-making reflect this notion of budgetary politics.

For this second conception of political influence, an agency may experience high levels of budgetary success at various reviewing levels because of carefully cultivated contacts, an image of reliability, or bargains struck much earlier. Civil servants at the departmental level or higher and politicians serving on various relevant political or legislative committees, in the Cabinet, or on the Council may intervene on the agency's behalf because they have been carefully cultivated by the agency in the past. That support may be forthcoming with scant connection to fundamental partisan cleavages in a programmatic sense. Thus, in the first case, agency budgetary success is closely tied to policy preferences of the several political parties; those agencies carrying out activities afforded a high level of priority among political parties are successful. There is no question here of bargaining, trade-offs, deference to administrative planners, or whatever. In the second case, agency budgetary success is a function of the support it receives from its alliances, both formal and informal, throughout the budgetary proceedings.

We should not overdraw the logical distinction between these two conceptions of the politics of budgeting. In the real world, their elements are certainly entertwined. Indeed, occupancy of positions on various governmental structures provides political parties with one kind of opportunity to shape important government decisions. An example, however, may help to illustrate how these alternative conceptions of the focus of political conflict manifest themselves in budgetary deliberations.

Consider the case where a substantial expansion of children's services for low income citizens is under consideration by municipal decision-makers. If the party programmatic conception of the politics of budgeting is the appropriate one, then what patterns of political conflict surrounding that policy and its funding would we expect to find? Members and leaders of political parties would be pursuing a variety of informal options available to them in efforts to support or oppose that proposal. In addition, party members would be expected to utilize their positions on various governmental structures – the Council Finance Committee, the layman political committees, the City Cabinet – as a base of influence to pursue their goals. But, since those structures are composed of representatives from several or all parties, no distinct view or orientation would develop around the structure itself. Statements such as 'the Council Finance Committee usually opposes the expansion of social welfare services while the layman political committees support such expansion' would not be very useful. It would not be useful because there would be no distinctive view or orientation attached to the structure; rather, each structure would reflect the natural diversity anticipated when members of opposing parties hold collegial positions on a given structure. In such instances, structures of government become important only as one of several resources available to political parties for shaping government decisions. A satisfactory explanation of the success or failure of that proposal would then devolve upon the stances taken by the political parties themselves.

This pattern would diverge substantially from the alliance structure conception of budgetary politics. It is implicit in that model that distinct orientations toward policy and spending develop around the structure itself which mute, in part, the diversity of opinions held by the occupants of those structural positions. For example, in the American case, it has become customary to speak of the House Appropriations Committee as the 'guardian of the public purse' and the Senate Appropriations Committee as an 'appeals court' – reflecting the implicit view that these distinct orientations toward issues of public spending cannot be accounted for by differences in party composition and party orientation.[6] Under these conditions, we would expect agency officials, intent upon the expansion of social services for children, to seek the support of, say, the Council Finance Committee and the Chief Municipal Administrator's office as structures which have exhibited a cutting bias in the past. And we would expect that the successes and failures of that effort would depend upon support afforded by these and other such structures in government. Occupants of various structural positions depart, in varying degrees, from party issue positions and come to hold more in common with their colleagues on those structures. The consequences of support from particular political parties become, under these conditions, secondary or insignificant.

The distinction between these two models of political effects on government decision is related to, but not equivalent to, more conventional discussions on the relative importance of bureaucratic politics and legislative politics for policy outcomes. In fact, the elements of the former may be seen as constituting a subset of the components of the alliance structure model described above. If we find that support from different government structures provides the key to budget success and, furthermore, that bureaucratic structures (in this case, the department head and the Chief Municipal Administrator) are the two most critical ones, then we would have said something of the importance of bureaucratic politics for government decisions. There is much in the research literature on government budgeting to support that restricted interpretation of the alliance structure model.

We believe, however, that some of the issues involved have been confused in prior research applications. The most conventional approach to dealing with these questions of the relative importance of bureaucracies, legislatures, and political parties in budgeting has been to examine the formal outputs of institutions and structures in government. It has become customary to observe, particularly for the parliamentary systems of Western Europe, that (1) formulation and alteration of budget requests by bureaucratic participants are significant and substantial; (2) formulation and alteration of budget requests by legislative participants are infrequent and insignificant; and (3) therefore, since legislatures institutionalize party conflict, the inference that political parties and legislatures play insignificant roles in public funding decisions is not a difficult one to draw. We believe that several issues become confused in arguments of this kind. The argument assumes, for example, that the effects of political parties on budgeting are accurately monitored in an examination of the formal outputs of the institution in which political parties are formally represented. We shall discuss the validity of that assumption and others later; but we may recast the problem in these terms momentarily and address the face validity of that argument about the relative importance of bureaucratic and legislative institutions for budget change.

Each agency formulates its budget request every year. As far as the formal changes are concerned, three municipal organs have the opportunity subsequently to alter that request before final appropriations for the agency become fixed: the department head, the Chief Municipal Administrator, and the City Council. The total change in that request may be partitioned into three components, each measuring the change that is due to action taken at each of these three levels. We define the following quantities for each year over n agencies:

Note here that we take the absolute value of the change at each level. Otherwise we would drastically underestimate the magnitude of change at the Council level, where it is customary to return a portion of funds deleted earlier in the review process.

These components for a nineteen-year period are plotted cumulatively in the graph in Figure 1. The bottom line in the graph shows the percentage of total agency requests altered by the department head. The middle line shows the percentage of total agency requests altered by the Chief Municipal Administrator and department head combined.

$$\frac{TC}{\sum_{i=1}^{n} w_i} = \frac{\sum_{i=1}^{n} |w-x|_i}{\sum_{i=1}^{n} w_i} + \frac{\sum_{i=1}^{n} |x-y|_i}{\sum_{i=1}^{n} w_i} + \frac{\sum_{i=1}^{n} |y-z|_i}{\sum_{i=1}^{n} w_i}$$

or

Total Percent change in agency requests = Percent change in agency requests at departmental level + Percent change in agency requests at CMA level + Percent change in agency requests at Council level

Figure 1

Decomposition of Total Change in Agency Requests into Three Components: Departmental Change, Chief Municipal Administrator Change, and Council Change, 1953-1971

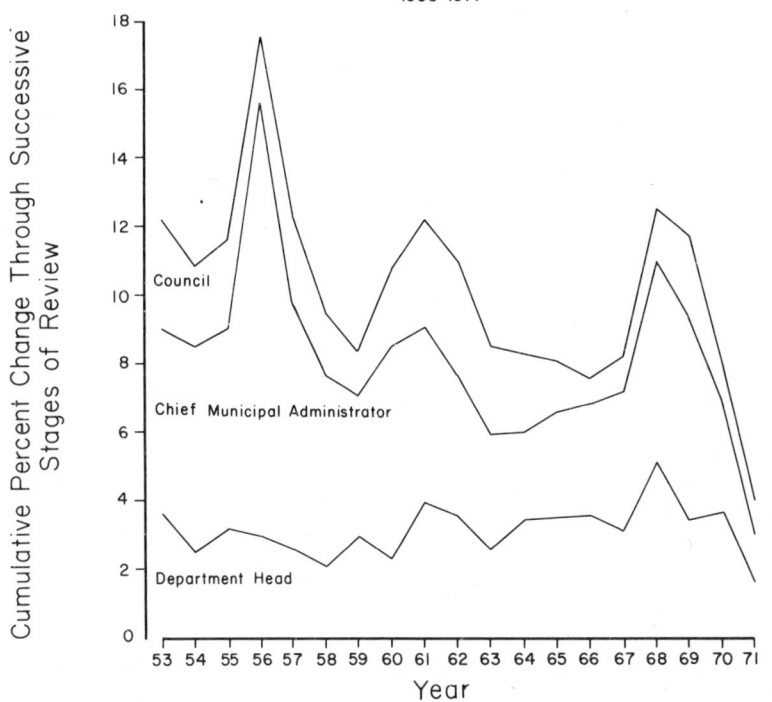

63

And the top line plots the total percentage change in original agency requests. Thus, the area between the three lines provides a visual impression of the relative importance of each level for the total budget change. It is reasonably clear that action by the two principal bureaucratic elements accounts for the bulk of changes made in original agency requests. For example, in 1953 total agency requests were altered in the range of 12 percent during the subsequent review process. Yet only about 3 percent can be attributed to Council action; the remaining 9 percent was concentrated at the two principal administrative levels – the department and the Chief Municipal Administrator's office. Although there is certainly not a one to one correspondence between these computations and the elements of the two models which we described above, these findings would seem to direct our thinking toward the view that the restricted interpretation of the alliance structure model is more appropriate than is the party programmatic model.

An examination of these components is certainly instructive on the question of the relative importance of administrative versus legislative institutions in budgeting. Furthermore, if we assume that legislatures institutionalize party conflict and bureaucracies institutionalize bureaucratic conflict, we might be inclined to infer something of the importance of political parties in budgeting from this kind of analysis. Yet, this kind of inference would surely lead to an understimate of effects for political parties on budgeting. The interrelationships between institutions would be ignored. The effects of political parties will not be adequately monitored by the formal outputs of the legislature. Indeed, more subtle effects may be evident from an assessment of the determinants of bureaucratic decisions as well.

The instances in which leaders of political parties or, more generally, members of elected legislatures contact government officials in support of various programs or proposals must surely be numerous. If such contacts are successful, then their effects will be felt, not in the formal legislative output, but rather at earlier points in the review process itself. We can well imagine that these kinds of partisan inputs to bureaucratic decision-making are sufficiently strong on occasion to alter the intended decision. These kinds of subtle effects are simply missed in an analysis of the formal outputs of legislative and bureaucratic institutions; and we believe that this kind of assumption underlies the findings of earlier studies of budgeting which attest to the minor or insignificant role of political parties and legislatures in budgeting. Furthermore, this kind of analysis disregards other structures of government simply because they do not bear formal responsibilities for final decisions at particular points in the process.

We believe, then, that these kinds of questions require a different mode of analysis. The question of the relative importance of bureaucratic politics versus partisan politics for resource allocation decisions remains an important one; but little will be learned of that with a restricted focus on the formal outputs of those respective government institutions. Rather, we shall deal with it from the standpoint of the two models of political effect set out above – the party programmatic model and the alliance structure model. For the remainder of this chapter, we shall assess the utility of the former for studying budgetary politics, reserving for Chapter V an assessment of the latter. We shall, at that point, be able to say something of the relative importance of each of these two conceptions of politics for budgeting.

Party Activism, Political Conflict, and Budgeting

Each of the seven national political parties in Norway has been active at the local level in Oslo: the Labor Party, the Socialist Peoples Party, the Communist Party, the Conservative Party, the Center Party, the Christian Peoples Party, the Liberal Party. The former three parties have normally constituted governments of the left, with the Labor Party being the dominant coalition partner; and the latter four parties have constituted governments of the right, with the Conservative Party holding the dominant coalition position in those governments. We have argued that an examination of the formal outputs of legislatures will lead to an underestimate of the significance of these political parties for budgeting. We suspect, rather, that the impact of partisan political machinations will be felt in the decisional outcomes of administrative/bureaucratic elements as well. This view leads naturally to an assessment, from an interorganizational perspective, of the informal contacts between bureaucracies and political parties. Indeed, it is that kind of informal contact – the occasional letter from important politicians to administrators, a telephone conversation at a critical point in the review process, personal conversations about the significance of some programs and the insignificance of others – which may provide political parties with the more important opportunities to shape resource allocation decisions.

If we are to conclude that the party programmatic conception of the politics of budgeting is the appropriate one, then more is involved than a simple assessment of the impact of party support on budget success. We cannot speak nebulously of the consequences of party support without saying something, as well, about the mechanisms by which those consequences are realized. In addition to the opportunities available to parties in the City Council to make alterations in government-proposed budgets, the informal contacts between politicians and bureaucrats, as we have suggested above, provide a second mechanism by which parties affect budgeting decisions. An assessment of model validity depends not only on the estimates of individual effects in these data but also on the discovery of structure among data. Thus, we begin by trying to understand the conditions under which parties become active on budgetary questions.

Given what is known of the kind of incremental determinism which pervades budgetary processes, it would be exceptionally naive to suggest that partisan controversies surround the spending decision process for every program in every agency and at every level of review. Many programs are first implemented, become accepted over a period of time as integral parts of government activity, and are rarely challenged by either politicians or administrators. That this is true for municipal politics in Oslo is suggested by the one-half of our respondents who fail to mention any political parties when asked about the frequency of party contact on their behalf during budgetary considerations. Given the vast range of municipal services, programs, and governmental units, there is simply no reason to anticipate that partisan imbroglios engulf them all. Political party activism in budgetary affairs is a variable itself which depends upon the extent of controversy over the activities of the governmental unit involved.

That this is so is indicated by the relationships shown in Table 1. Respondents were asked to name those political parties which were likely to intervene on their behalf at various points during the process of budget review. We define party activism for a given agency as the number of parties mentioned (ranging from 0 to 4). The remaining variables in Table 1 are alternative measures of political conflict over agency activities: R's estimate of the level of political priority afforded the activities of his agency (ranging from 0 to 10); R's estimate of the extent of agreement between socialist and bourgeois parties on that priority setting (ranging from 0 to 10); and R's estimate of the percentage of his total budget spent on non-controversial activities.

The relationships between these measures of perceived political conflict and party activism are uniformly significant and sizeable. Political parties become active in the budget review process for agencies in which public monies are spent on controversial activities and for which there is much disagreement between socialist and bourgeois parties over the level of priority which should be given to those activities. These patterns provide confirmation of some initial conditions relevant to the party programmatic model of political effects. Political parties do utilize informal channels in efforts to shape resource allocation decisions, but a major stimulant to that effort is the controversial nature of agency activities.

Table 1. Party Activism in Budgeting and Political Conflict*

	Socialist/Bourgeois Agreement on Level of Political Priority	% Budget going to non-controversial activities	Party Activism
Level of Political Priority	+0.494*	+0.407*	-0.305*
Socialist/Bourgeois Agreement on Level of Political Priority		+4.82*	-0.427*
% Budget going to non-controversial activities			-0.396*

* Statistically significant at .05 level or better; n × 53.

* Question wording: 'Would you say that the activities of your agency are given a high level of political priority by the administrative and political leadership in Oslo, or would you say that priority is rather low?' (0 to 10 scale response) 'To what extent is there agreement between the socialist and nonsocialist parties on that?' (0 to 10 scale response) 'We understand that many of the activities of your agency are widely accepted and supported by the municipal leadership in Oslo and, as such, don't generate much controversy when your budget proposals are put forward; others seem more controversial. About what percentage of the funds in your budget proposal for the upcoming year would you say involve such noncontroversial items?' (record actual percentage) 'Are there any parties' representatives who are likely to work actively in support of your agency when your budget proposals are under consideration?' (Code number of parties mentioned).

It is likely, however, that the stimulants to party activism on budgetary matters lie not only in properties internal to the agency itself – e.g. the controversiality of programs, activities, budgets – but also in some important characteristics of the parties involved. While a number of other attributes of parties may be important, these data allow us to treat at least two such attributes: party size and party location along a left-right continuum. It is a fact of life for five of these seven political parties that they are small in number. Literally in terms of manpower, their efforts would have to be voluminous to match the frequency of contacts or budget interventions by the two largest parties – the Labor Party and the Conservative Party.

That party size serves as a real constraint on party activism in budgeting is indicated by the percentage entries in Table 2. The first row of that table shows the percentage of all party mentions for a given party when respondents were asked which parties were likely to intervene on their behalf. The second row shows the size of each party as measured by its representation in the City Council. Clearly the two largest parties – the Labor Party and the Conservative Party – are the most active from the standpoint of interventions during the process of budget considerations.

The differences between these two distributions for each party is strongly suggestive of a second determinant of party activism in budgetary matters. First, the parties are arranged in Table 2 in an order consistent with the traditional left-right distinction. The Socialist People's Party is the farthest to the left of these parties, and the Conservative Party is the farthest to the right. We shall provide validating evidence below for this particular ordering; but if we accept this ordering for our present purposes, it is apparent that the left parties are more active and the right parties less active than would be predicted solely on the basis of their size. Indeed, the Conservative Party stands out here clearly as the dominant bourgeois party, on the one hand, but remarkably less active than its size would indicate.

It is natural that left-wing parties are more active on questions of government spending than are right-wing parties. First, the context in which these interventions take place is almost always one in which bureaucratic reviewers are deleting funds from agency requests. The department heads and the Chief Municipal Administrator rarely leave a

Table 2. Party Size and Party Activism in Budgeting*

	Socialist People's Party	Labor Party	Liberal Party	Center Party	Christian People's Party	Conservative Party	(N)
Party Activism: Percentage of all mentions	16%	47%	12%	2%	4%	20%	(54)
Party Size: Percentage of Seats in Council	8%	42%	4%	2%	6%	37%	(83)
Difference	+8%	+5%	+8%	0%	-2%	-17%	

* The Communist Party is excluded, since it held no seats on the City Council; one indepedent socialist and one non-political representative are excluded from the Council seat distribution.

requested budget intact. The net effect of their alterations is to diminish government spending and, thus, to limit the role of government in society from what it otherwise might have been. Left-wing parties, in contrast, favor an expanded role of government in society and a concomitant increase in spending across a range of policy areas. Thus, the heightened activism of left-wing parties during the budgetary review process would be fully expected from considerations of this kind.

Party Support and Budget Success

Political parties become active in the budget affairs of controversial agencies. They do so by interceding through a variety of informal contacts with higher level officials who review agency budgets. Larger political parties are generally more active than are smaller political parties, but parties on the left are more active and parties on the right less active than would be expected solely on the basis of their size. But what are the consequences of this kind of activity? Are such effects concentrated on such marginal quantities of larger agency budgets that the ramifications for overall budget expansion and success become trivial? Furthermore, what factors seem to divide the parties in terms of the agencies to which they afford budget support? In particular, is the traditional left-right dimension of government involvement in society operative in budgetary politics as well?

We sought to tap the concept of political party support for agency activities. We could, however, have pursued at least two alternative measurement strategies here. Agency officials could be asked about their perception of support from each of the seven political parties; or, members of the political parties could be interviewed and asked about their actual support for each of these agencies. At first glance the latter strategy may be thought to produce the more reliable results. In that case we would be dealing, not with statements about perceptions of party support, but rather with actual statements of support by the supporters. Recall, however, that we are dealing with nearly fifty agencies; and it seems unlikely that each of these seven political parties develop specific stances about the value of the activities of so large a number of individual agencies. Party support is likely to be much more situation specific. We suspect that a more reliable estimate of that support can be obtained by asking each agency official about the supportiveness of the seven political parties than by asking party members to engage in the exhaustive task of evaluating nearly fifty agencies. These responses are more likely to reflect the actual cumulative experiences of the agency, over a period of time, with the political parties involved. Thus, we rely on individual agency officials to tell us something of the support or opposition provided by each of the seven political parties as regards his own agency.

Respondents were given a list of the seven political parties – the Labor Party, the Conservative Party, the Liberal Party, the Christian People's Party, the Center Party, the Socialist People's Party, and the Communist Party. Each was asked to evaluate, on a scale ranging from 0 to 10, the consistency of each party's viewpoints or programs with his own conception of his agency's goals. Each respondent recorded his evaluations in a matrix, box-like presentation – a procedure which we felt forced his relative positioning of parties to stand out more clearly to him. We have, then, an estimate of support afforded each agency by each of the seven political parties; and we may probe these observations further to understand the dimensions which divide these parties in terms of agencies supported as well as the consequences of that support.

While other cleavages in Norwegian politics have come and gone, one enduring basis of conflict among political parties remains: the question of the appropriate level of government involvement in society or the traditional left-right dimension. The three socialist parties have argued, in varying degrees, for an expanded role of government in society; and the four bourgeois parties, in equally varying degrees, have preferred more limited government involvement. We have seen some of the empirical manifestations of that ideological distinction in terms of party efforts to assist agencies on questions of budget expansion.

Converse and Valen have provided evidence which indicates that the left-right dimension is a potent one for national electoral evaluations in Norway.[7] It is not obvious, however, that such a dimension is equally operative in municipal budgetary politics. First, electorates may perceive much sharper differences among political parties than actually exist in terms of party behavior in government. Second, as we move from national politics with a more diverse constituency to local politics with a less diverse constituency, the dimensions of conflict may be altered considerably; and the key may lie in consensus, rather than in the differences, among all parties. In either event, the expectation would be that salient dimensions for the national electorate would be much restrained for the actual activities of party in government at the municipal level.

The evaluations by agency officials of the seven political parties were submitted to a multidimensional scaling routine; the results are shown in Figure 2.[8] Dimension II divides the seven political parties neatly on a coalition basis – the four bourgeois parties located in the upper portion of the graph and the three socialist parties in the lower portion. This is the traditional basis of coalitions in Norway, and it is natural that these responses pick up such a distinction. Variations along Dimension II are not immediately interpretable beyond that point.[9]

It is, however, Dimension I which provides us with the richer set of information on the subtleties of the left-right dimension for party in government in Oslo. This traditional left-right dimension appears to be operative much as it has been shown to be for the Norwegian electorate as a whole. The Communist Party and the Socialist People's Party lie on the extreme left and are similar in terms of agency supportiveness. While both are somewhat distant from their dominant coalition partner, the Labor Party, all three are positioned clearly on the left.

The four traditional bourgeois coalition partners – the Liberal Party, the Center Party, the Christian People's Party, and the Conservative Party – are appropriately located to the right of the three socialist parties. The Conservative Party – the dominant coalition party and the most conservative – is found on the extreme right. The positioning of the Liberal Party slightly to the left of the neutral point is an interesting one. In spite of its efforts to move to the left in recent years, it continues to appear safely on the right in multidimensional scaling routines based upon national electoral evaluations. Such movement, however, seems to have been picked up more sharply by governmental elites. While the Liberal Party remains safely to the right of the three socialist parties, it is somewhat similar to those parties from the standpoint of agency support.

Figure 2. Dimensions of Political Party Support

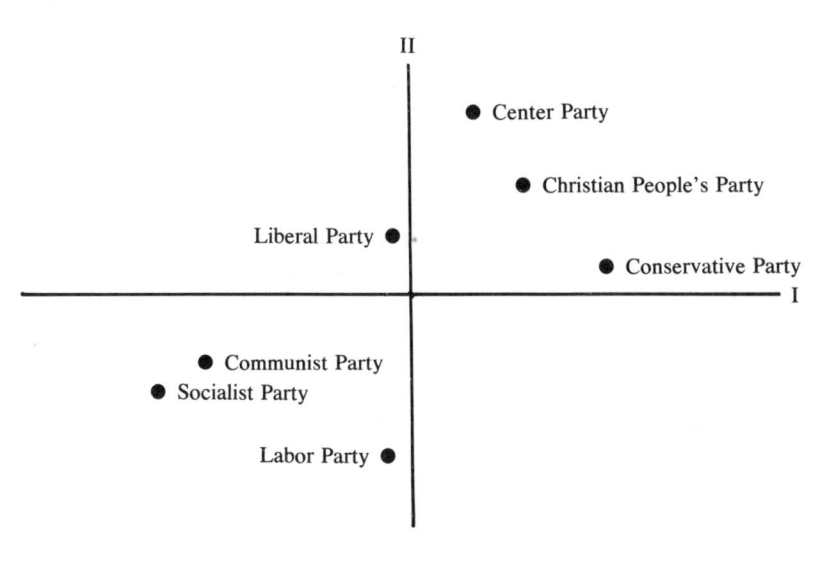

Both the traditional clustering on a coalition basis and more subtle variations along the left-right continuum divide the seven political parties into two groups. Some agency officials draw much of their budgetary support (or opposition) from the bourgeois parties on the right; others depend upon the socialist parties on the left. It appears, then, that the left-right dimension – government involvement in society – serves to differentiate political parties in terms of the government agencies to which they afford support. Thus, with some understanding of the determinants of party activism in budgeting and the dimensions along which the parties divide on such questions, we may move to an assessment of the consequences of that support.

The hypothesis that support for individual agency goals from each of the political parties importantly affects the fortunes of agency budgets may be formalized as follows:

$$S_{qi} = a_0 + \sum_{j=1}^{7} a_j x_{ji} + e_i$$

where

S_q = budgetary acquisitiveness or success with $q=1, \ldots, 9$ according to the particular formulation of the dependent variable.

x_{ji} = agency official i's positive/negative evaluation of party j, on a scale from 0 to 10.

and the a_j's are regression parameters to be estimated.

Thus, we conceive of agency budget acquisitiveness or success as linear combinations of the estimated level of support from each of the seven political parties. The question is then how well the variations in those decisions across agencies can be accounted for by taking account of that support (or opposition).

Table 3 shows the results from conceiving of each of these dependent variables as linear functions of party support. The squared multiple correlation coefficients are uniformly significant and attest to the importance of partisan political support for budgetary decisions at each stage in the process. Indeed, for perhaps the best measure of overall success (appropriations as a percentage of the original agency request), over half of the variance in budgetary success is explained by the level of programmatic support afforded an agency by the political parties themselves. It is no accident that the weakest of these relationships is found at the point of Council decision on the government-proposed budget — an observation which lends support to our earlier feeling that the importance of political parties would not necessarily be reflected in the formal output of legislative institutions.

While the results of these multiple regression formulations are indicative of the relatively high explanatory power of party support variables for budget success, they deal rather inelegantly with the subtleties of variation among the parties. For this time period (and the decade before), the socialist parties have held the majority in municipal elections and in Council representation. Thus, support from the

Table 3. Budgetary Change as Linear Functions of Support from Seven Political Parties

Dependent Variable	Squared Multiple Correlation Coefficient
Level Specific Budget Change:	
dept rec/agen req	.472*
CMA rec/dept rec	.554*
Coun app/CMA rec	.390*
Cumulative Budget Change:	
dept rec/agen req	.472*
CMA rec/agen req	.611*
Coun rec/agen req	.552*
Appropriations Increase Budget Change:	
agen req/prior app	.508*
dept rec/prior app	.482*
CMA rec/prior app	.476*
Coun app/prior app	.461*

* Statistically significant at .05 level; n = 50.

bourgeois parties may have become much less critical for budget success. The key party support variable may be simply the level of support provided by the dominant left coalition partner — the Labor Party. Furthermore, we have provided evidence earlier of important differences between the socialist and bourgeois party groups on budgetary matters: (1) the socialist parties are more likely to intervene during the budget review process than are the bourgeois parties; and (2) the left-right dimension divides the socialist parties from the bourgeois parties in terms of the kinds of agencies to which they afford support in budgetary matters. These multiple linear regression formulations serve to obscure rather than reveal important distinctions of this kind.

Inferences drawn from our earlier presentations are ambiguous on this point. The strong positive correlation in Table 1 between the level of priority afforded an agency's activities and the level of agreement between socialist and bourgeois parties on that priority setting would seem to suggest that the most successful agencies are those who have solidified support from both party groups. In Table 2, however, we noted the markedly higher activism of left-wing parties on matters of budgeting – suggesting that support from the left may provide more payoffs than support from the right. Thus, it is not clear at this point which party groups appear to play a pivotal role in budgeting.

We may return to our ordering of parties along the left-right dimension to answer these kinds of questions. Imagine, first, that we take account of variations in support only by the most left-wing of parties – the Communist Party. The dependent variable, budget success, may be treated as a linear function of the level of support from that party. The resulting squared correlation coefficient would then indicate the proportion of the total variance in budget success explained by support from the Communist Party, Second, however, support from the next most left-wing of parties would be added to that regression equation; and the variance explained by considerations of support from these two most left-wing of parties could be assessed. In similar fashion we move successively rightward on the left-right continuum – adding one party to the regression equation at a time and examining resulting proportions of variance explained by the inclusion of each additional party.

Our purpose in such an exercise is to answer the question whether both socialist and bourgeois parties play a critical role in budget success of individual agencies or whether the key to budget success lies only in support from the socialist majority – particularly, the dominant Labor Party. If the latter is true, then the estimate of variance explained in budget success by political party support should approach a maximum with the inclusion in the regression equation of the first three parties on the left. The subsequent inclusion of each additional (bourgeois) party support variable should result in trivial increments to explained variance. If, on the other hand, the bourgeois parties continue to play a vital role in budgetary affairs, then increments to explained variance with the addition of those party support variables should be more dramatic. We may think in terms of representing these estimates of variance explained graphically from left to right. The first point plotted would be the estimate of explained variance by the support of the Communist Party alone. The final point plotted would be the comparable figure for support from all seven political parties. Intermediate points would show those estimates for the inclusion of each additional party, moving from left to right. If support from the dominant left-wing majority coalition is the key to budget success, then the line would assume a logarithmic form with a negative second derivative and a positive first derivative which approaches zero at the third point on the party location scale (i.e., the inclusion of support by the first three socialist parties). If, on the other hand, the posture of the bourgeois parties remains important for budget success, the estimates of variance explained with the addition of each party could assume any of several forms graphically (e.g., linear or parabolic), but the slopes would continue to be positive beyond the point of inclusion of the Labor Party.

The graph in Figure 3 portrays results in this fashion. Utilizing the measure of overall budget success – appropriations as a percentage of original agency request – seven separate regression analyses were performed, each differing from the earlier by the inclusion of one additional party support variable according to the left-right ordering of parties. Support from the two small socialist parties is negligibly related to budget success. Rather, a first clear plateau is reached with the inclusion of support by the Labor Party. Nearly one-fourth of the variance in overall budget success can be accounted for by considering

Figure 3

Variance Explained in Budget Success by Successive Inclusion of Each Additional Party From Left to Right in Regression Equation

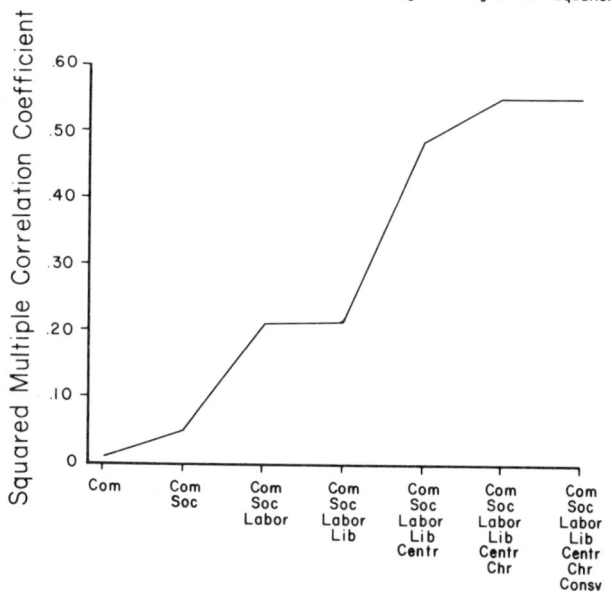

Party Support Variables Included in Regression Equation

only the support or opposition provided by the socialist majority; and most of that can be attributed to the posture of the dominant coalition partner, the Labor Party. Yet, the estimates of variance explained in Figure 3 show that a second plateau is reached with the inclusion of support and opposition of the bourgeois parties as well. Apparently the three most conservative parties play a pivotal role in the more informal aspects of budget considerations; indeed, the proportion of variance explained is doubled by the inclusion of the support and opposition variables of these bourgeois parties.

The posture of the bourgeois parties becomes important in two respects. First, a consensus between socialist and bourgeois coalitions on the value of a governmental unit's activities insures a high level of budget success. It is apparently difficult for administrative budget reviewers to delete significant items from agency budgets when that agency enjoys the support of all seven political parties. A second kind of effect of the bourgeois coalition is the depressing effect which it can have on expenditure decisions. That negative, non-supportive inputs may account for the bulk of the potency of the bourgeois minority in

Figure 4

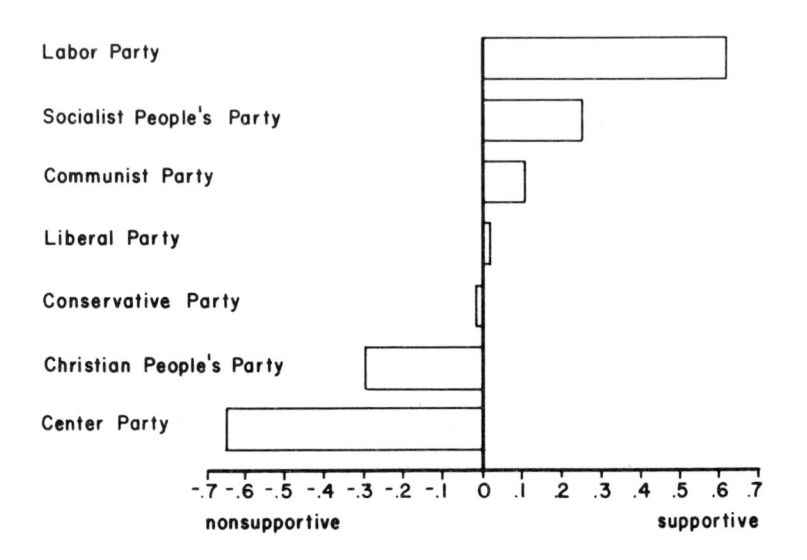

Party Supportiveness: Grand Means of Deviations from Individual Means

budget questions is suggested by Figure 4. Here each individual's mean across the seven party support variables is computed and then subtracted from his raw score response for each party. The overall means are then computed for those adjusted scores. Negative means indicate that a given party is generally seen as less supportive than is the average party. The resulting histogram of adjusted means in Figure 4 suggests that the bourgeois parties are almost always seen as less supportive of agency goals than are the socialist parties. Thus, their input into budgetary decision points may be more frequently aimed at reducing the level of government spending across a significant number of governmental units. In spite of their minority status, however, that input is apparently a potent one.

Conclusions: Budgeting and Party Politics

The party programmatic conception of the politics of budgeting holds that political parties take distinguishable stands on questions of resource allocation, that those parties engage in efforts – both formal and informal – designed to insure the realization of those preferences, and that the consequences of those efforts are reflected in the actual decisional outputs of government institutions. There is much in the structure of these data which yields validity to that view of the politics of budgeting. We have tried to rely on patterns of relationships rather than on particular relationships in assessing model validity. In effect, we have looked for structure among data by examining several sets of relationships which give empirical plausibility to that more general interpretation.

The importance of political parties for budgeting will not be monitored very well by an examination of the formal outputs of legislatures – the governmental structure in which partisan conflict is institutionalized. Rather, as bureaucracies come to play larger roles in dealing with complex questions of budget formulation and review, the focus for party influence is likely to shift. As a result of these kinds of informal influence attempts, the effects of party interventions will be felt in the decisional outputs of bureaucracies as well as in the formal outputs of legislatures. That this is so is reflected in the ability of the party support variables to account for a substantial proportion of the variance in budget success for bureaucratic as well as legislative decisions.

Political parties do not, however, become perturbed over all questions of government spending. Indeed, we do not view such a condition as even a necessary one for model validity. Party activism in budgetary affairs is a varible itself which fluctuates with the degree of controversy surrounding the activities of different governmental units. It is the budgets of controversial agencies which attract the attentions and interventions of party members. Still, support from political parties in Oslo contributes measurably to agency budget success at each step in the review process. We are able to account for over one half of the variance in overall success in steering requests through successive levels of review by treating that success as a linear function of support from the seven political parties.

The importance of the left-right dimension of government involvement in society has been apparent at several points in our analysis. First, budgetary interventions in support of agency budget expansion are more frequent for parties on the left than for parties on the right – a natural reflection of the former's preference for an expanded role for government in society. Second, there appear to be real differences – as reflected in the views of agency officials about political parties – in the kinds of agencies supported by the socialist and bourgeois parties. A multidimensional representation of the similarities and differences among those parties reveals a consistent left-right ordering of the parties in terms of agency supportiveness.

Finally, although the socialist parties hold the majority, the bourgeois minority is not of trivial importance in budgeting decisions. While the bourgeois minority could not be expected to carry important votes on questions of government spending in the Council, its more subtle effects on earlier stages in the budget review process are quite evident. While support from the dominant socialist majority accounts for about one-fourth of the variance in overall budget success, that proportion is doubled by the subsequent inclusion of support (opposition) variables from the remaining bourgeois parties. Since these officials generally see the bourgeois parties as much less supportive than the socialist parties, it is likely that the net effect of bourgeois party activity is to hold government spending down from what it otherwise might have been.

The conflicts, controversies, compromises, and agreements among political parties thus seem to constitute an important focus for the politics of budgeting in Oslo. That a substantial proportion of the variance in budget success can be accounted for by examining the level of party support for each agency is testimony to that view. Yet, political parties are certainly not formally represented at the most important stages of budget formulation and review. Indeed, much of our evidence thus far on the politics of budgeting rests on assumptions about intricate informal mechanisms and networks of association – intricacies for which these data do only partial justice. As budget work has become more complex, new structures and institutions have grown up around major bureaucratic decision points. Since formal decisions in bureaucracies account for the bulk of budget changes, lower level officials may have come to concentrate their efforts on those structures and institutions – presumably on the assumption that these municipal organs or individuals constitute the more important focus for budgetary politics. We shall, then, turn to an examination of the validity of that conception of the politics of budgeting – the alliance structure model – in the following chapter.

V. The Politics of Budgeting: Alliance Structure Politics

One of the most important properties associated with the expansion of government is the proliferation in the number of governmental structures which either participate formally or are consulted informally during the taking of important government decisions. The department head and his staff come to play a critical role in budget deliberations; members of the City Cabinet may develop hostile or supportive views about the actions of bureaucratic reviewers; the Council Finance Committee produces a set of budget recommendations which may diverge from the wishes of members of other governmental structures. Our focus thus far on the four points at which budgetary decisions are actually made obscures the potential importance of a number of other government structures which participate as well. With the growth in the number of such participating structures, we may expect to find an increasing preoccupation by lower level officials with securing the support of those structures in the budget review process.

It is this view of the politics of budgeting which underlies the alliance structure model of political effects. Elites holding positions on these various structures develop views about the issues of public spending consonant with the views of their colleagues serving on those same structures. The important bases of conflict on resource allocation no longer center on partisan political controversies. Rather, conflict centers on preference disparities among different institutions and structures within government. Under these conditions lower level officials direct their efforts toward gaining the support of particular governmental structures on budgetary questions.

Layman political committees, for example, have been established alongside a number of these agencies, and one of the tasks of those committees is to review the budget request of the agency and to make recommendations to higher level officials. It is not unusual to find a supporter of the Conservative Party and a supporter of the Labor Party serving on the same committee. These committees are ordinarily quite supportive of agency efforts at budget expansion. The Council Finance

Committee, similarly composed of members of opposing parties, is, however, typically less supportive of budget expansion efforts. The alliance structure model of political effects holds that the gaining of support from these alternative structures is more important for budget success than is the acquisition of support from political parties whose members may or may not serve on those structures. Conservatives and Laborites alike on the layman political committees may support the budget expansion efforts of 'their' agency while action by the Council Finance Committee may suggest across-the-board opposition.

Studies of budgeting in the American national government provide some support for this view of the politics of budgeting. Agency officials are said to seek the support of various structures in government – the department heads, the Office of Management and Budget, the Presidency. Even though party composition is similar, the two Appropriations Committees in Congress develop their own characteristic behaviors; the House Appropriations Committee may introduce substantial cuts into budget requests while the Senate Appropriations Committee returns a portion of those deleted funds.[1] Presumably party composition cannot account for the differences in roles – 'guardian of the public purse' versus 'appeals court' – suggested by the behavior of those two structures.

In such instances the bases of conflict over issues of public spending shift. Different views about the appropriateness of expansion or curtailment of expenditures become associated with different structures in government; the politics of budgeting then becomes a process of building up support from several potential alliance elements in the budget review process; and the key to budget success for government agencies lies in the acquisition of support from those structures. The gaining of support from particular political parties becomes secondary, or even trivial. An empirical assessment of the validity of these two models of political effect allows us, then, to answer the broader question: Is the politics of resource allocation better understood as a process of conflict, compromise, and support among different governmental structures or among different political parties?

Perceptions of Alliance Elements

It would be unusual if officials dealt with various structures of government year after year but failed to develop coherent perceptions and expectations about the behavior of the occupants of those structural positions. Many agency officials come to expect sizeable deletions from their budgets. But some reviewers are heroes and others are villains; furthermore, the same reviewer may be seen as a hero by some and a villain by others. Yet, alliances cannot be formed and support obtained solely on the basis of such black and white views of human behavior. While the critical point may be the actual support an official receives from these municipal organs, support is only one element of serveral relevant perceptual properties. We shall examine three such properties which we believe to be central to the formation of alliances in budgeting. In that way, we hope to develop a picture of how these agency officials view the structures of government with which they must deal; and, on the assumption that these perceptions are reasonably accurate reflections of reality, we shall be able to say something about the roles of those structures in budgeting.

While each of these seven structures will have some say in budget decisions at some point in the review process, there is certainly no equitable distribution of influence across those structures. Some will be able to make final decisions while others will only have input to those decisions. Some will decide important questions about the budgets of all agencies, while others will engage in occasional interventions for some agencies. The extent to which a given structure is perceived to be influential in budget proceedings will have obvious implications for efforts to obtain its support. Presumably all agency officials would prefer to have the support of the more influential elements. This does not mean, however, that less influential elements are peripheral in alliance formation. Since access is likely to be more difficult in the case of influential elements, the less influential structures may come to constitute important elements of alliance structures.

A second perceptual property which we wish to examine is the competence of these participating structures in doing an adequate job of budget review. Much hostility in budgeting is generated by the view of lower level officials that higher level reviewing agents do not have the competence, resources, or expertise to review adequately their budget requests. We suspect that this is especially a problem for expressly political bodies in budgeting. Thus, we want to assess the perceived competence of these structural participants in budgeting.

A final property which we shall examine in somewhat greater detail is the level of support afforded each agency by each of these seven elements. While the first two properties – perceived influence and perceived competence for a given structure – are likely to reveal much greater conformity in evaluation across agency officials, the question of support is likely to be much more variable. Certain agencies will receive consistent support from some of these elements but not from others. The pattern may be the reverse for other agencies. We shall first assess the level of overall supportiveness of the seven structures in budgeting; next, we shall examine the similarities and dissimilarities of these structures in terms of the agencies to which they afford support or opposition, leaving to the last portion of this chapter the question of the consequences of that support for budget success.

The instruments utilized in measuring these three properties – influence, competence, and support – are similar to those utilized in measuring party support in the previous chapter. Respondents were presented with a matrix format listing these seven structures on the lefthand side – the department head, the Chief Municipal Administrator, the City Council, the Council Finance Committee, the Cabinet, the Mayor, and the relevant layman political committee. Each structure was then evaluated, on a scale from 0 to 10, with regard to its level of influence exerted in budgetary matters. That exercise was repeated at a later point on the questionnaire, this time on the basis of the adequacy of resources to review competently budgetary requests. Finally, a third comparable task was presented to respondents in which they evaluated the extent to which each structure was usually 'on their side' or not in budgetary controversies.

The graphs in Figure 1 show the means for adjusted scores for each set of evaluations. Since some respondents may have utilized different portions of the range of the scale, we first compute a respondent's individual mean across the seven responses for a given set of evaluations; that mean is then subtracted from the raw scores. Grand means are then computed for these adjusted scores across all respondents. The resulting graphs in Figure 1 provide a reasonable composite picture of how lower level officials evaluate the relative influence, competence, and support of the structures with which they must deal in budgetary questions.

Influence and competence in budgeting differentiate agency officials' evaluations of administrative structures from their evaluations of political structures. Only one of the five structures composed of politicians appears to be seen as very influential in budgeting – the Council Finance Committee. Neither the City Council, the Mayor, the City Cabinet, nor the layman political committees is viewed as being very influential on budgetary questions. Furthermore, none of these political structures even approximates the perceived level of competence in handling budgetary problems exhibited by the two bureaucratic participants – the department heads and the Chief Municipal Administrator. Indeed, this is one of the dilemmas which arises when political structures are created and designed for maintaining some control over important government decisions. Their resources are rarely sufficient to legitimize their involvement in those decision processes – at least as viewed by lower level officials; and the level of influence they exert appears insignificant in comparison to that of bureaucrats whose decisions they are supposed to influence. But we ought not to make too much of that perceived disparity between the characteristics of administrative and political structures. While the influence of any one political structure may be seen as marginal in an overall sense, the multiplicity of political structures may provide opportunities for more substantial influence in a net sense.

The question of perceived support from these alternative structures is more difficult to answer. Here the greatest disparities appear when the means for the two administrative structures are compared. A high level of support is most common from an agency official's department head and least common from the Chief Municipal Administrator. The role of the layman political committees is clearly a supportive one; but the value of that support is presumably reduced by the low level of influence exerted by those bodies. The tension between the views of the Council Finance Committee and the whole Council are evident – the former apparently being a much more likely foe than the latter.

From an agency official's viewpoint, the most positive alliance element is apparently the department head. The department heads are viewed as one of the most influential elements in budgetary matters. Furthermore, that exceptional level of influence is afforded a certain legitimacy by these officials: the resources of the department head and his staff are seen as quite sufficient to do competent budget work. The coupling of these two properties with the exceptional level of support

Figure 1

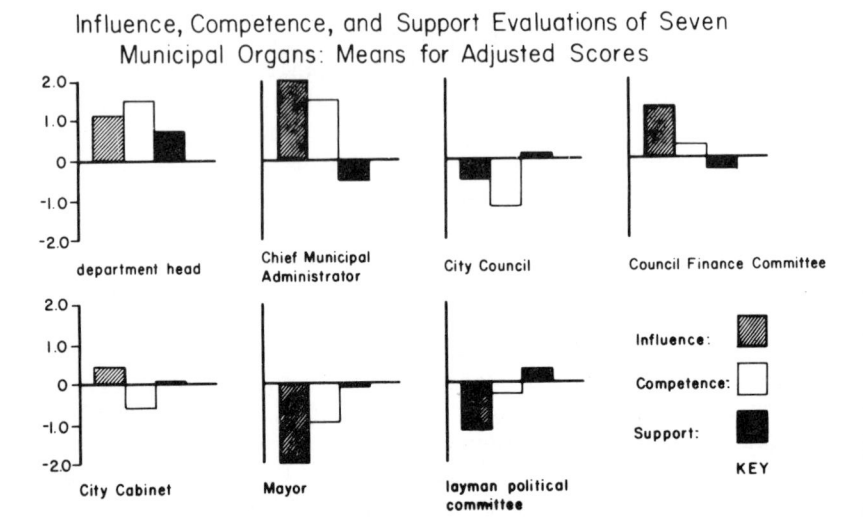

Influence, Competence, and Support Evaluations of Seven Municipal Organs: Means for Adjusted Scores

which apparently flows from departmental reviewers means that the departmental structure is seen as a rather important alliance component. This does not mean, of course, that the magnitude of departmental cuts of budget requests is trivial; indeed; those cuts are sizeable as Figure 1 in Chapter IV indicates. But much of that is undoubtedly anticipated, since the perceived level of support remains high.

Evaluations of the Chief Municipal Administrator's role in budgeting diverge more sharply across these three evaluative dimensions. The dilemma for lower level officials in their relationship with the office which prepares the final government-proposed budget is evident: that office is viewed as the most influential but the least supportive element in budgeting. Ordinarily much hostility might be generated by two such contrasting views. But much of that potential hostility is undoubtedly mitigated by the parallel view that actions at that level are competent and legitimate. The development of technical resources and expertise in these offices not only facilitates actual budget work but also affords a certain legitimacy to budget changes which are often dramatic indeed.

These support means, however, may obscure one of the most significant properties of alliance formation: all agencies need not benefit from the support or suffer from the opposition of the same structural participants in budgeting. Some agencies may find their support on budgetary matters concentrated, by and large, in the offices of the department head and the Chief Municipal Administrator. Others may be treated quite severely by those participants and, as a result, may be led to rely on favorable action by the Council in restoring depleted funds. While something of the overall orientation of these bodies is revealed by these means for supportiveness, such variations and disparities in the patterns of support and opposition are concealed.

It is not sufficient, however, simply to say or to observe that different agencies draw support and opposition from different structures and institutions in government. This kind of statement posits little more than a kind of random model of alliance formation and, specifically, predicts no structure or relationships between support and opposition from different alliance elements. Rather, we suspect that there are systematic patterns in the formation of alliances in budgeting which inhere in the characteristics of government institutions and structures themselves. We may approach the question of disparities in support and opposition among different structures in budgeting by asking initially how similar or dissimilar each structure is to other structures. If the relationship between agency officials' evaluations of support from the Council Finance Committee and support from the Chief Municipal Administrator is strong and positive, then those two structures would seem to be quite similar in terms of the agencies which they support and those which they oppose. If, on the other hand, that relationship is non-existent or negative, then those structures would appear to be rather unlike each other from the standpoint of agencies supported.

We are not interested solely, however, in these similarities and dissimilarities among potential alliance elements in budgeting; an understanding of the formation of alliances requires an understanding of the dimensions upon which alliances are based. We referred earlier, for example, to the perceived differences between administrative and political structures on questions of influence and competence; and we suspect that this distinction permeates the actual formation of alliances as well. Some lower level officials are likely to concentrate their efforts on familiar administrative elements (e.g., the department head, the Chief Municipal Administrator) – venturing rarely into the realm of legislative politics (e.g. the City Council, the Council Finance Committee). Other, more astute politicos may well cultivate the support of more manifestly political bodies. It is useful, then, to think in terms of mapping these similarities among alternative alliance elements into multidimensional space. By examining that resulting representation, we may then be able to infer something of the dimensions which shape the formation of alliances in budgeting.

Figure 2. Dimensions of Alliance Structure Support

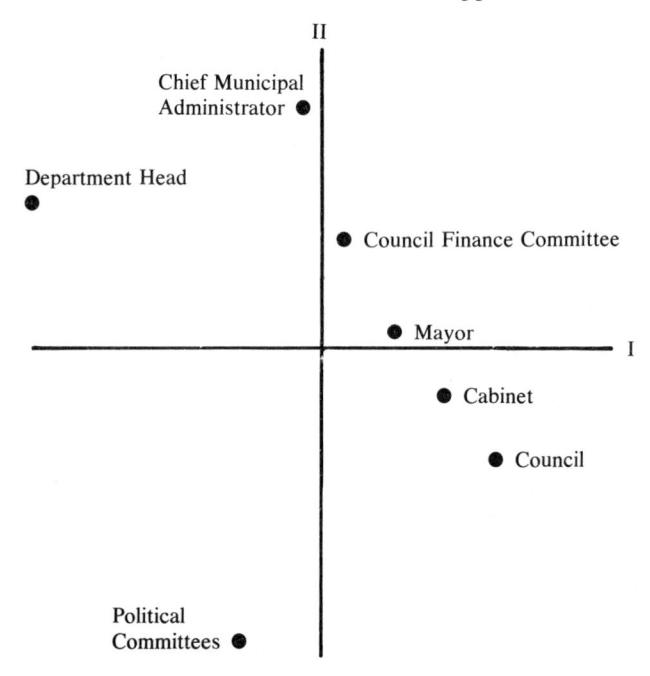

Pearson product-moment correlation coefficients were computed for each pair of support evaluations across the seven structures evaluated by these respondents. A strong positive coefficient between the support evaluations for two given structures indicates a marked similarity in terms of agencies supported. That intercorrelation matrix was submitted to a non-metric multidimensional scaling routine.[2] The results are shown in Figure 2:[3]

Our earlier observations concerning the differences between structures composed of politicians and structures composed of bureaucrats are similarly reflected in these results. With some perturbations, Dimension I may be interpreted as an administrative-political dimension in alliance formation. A projection of points onto Dimension I shows the department head – the most distinctly administrative or bureaucratic element among these structures – at one extreme and the City Council – the most distinctly partisan political body – at the other extreme. Intermediate locations of remaining structures could have been anticipated from some prior knowledge about the kinds of activities in which those structures engage. While there is little doubt that the Cabinet, the Mayor, and the Council Finance Committee are political bodies – in the sense of being composed of elected politicians –, their opportunities for engaging in some administrative kinds of activities (e.g. supervision, control, review) are greater than would be the case for an amorphous body of eightyfive politicians on the City Council; their intermediate locations on Dimension I are natural from that standpoint. The ambiguous stance of the Chief Municipal Administrator, a civil servant, is evident here. Although clearly on the 'administrative' side of Dimension I, his central role in preparing the government-proposed budget apparently places him at closer proximity to the political bodies with which he must deal.

These locations along Dimension I lend support to the view that one of the factors which shape the formation of alliances in budgeting inheres in the characteristics of the structures themselves. Some lower level officials rely, for the most part, on support from familiar administrative elements in the process (e.g. the department head, the Chief Municipal Administrator) – venturing rarely or not at all into the arena of legislative politics. Others, more capable of operating in expressly political environments, seek the support of more expressly political bodies (e.g. the Council, the Cabinet). That such a dimension separates some agency officials from others is suggested by the distances in Figure 2 between, for example, the department head and the City Council. An agency official who views the Council and the Cabinet as quite supportive of his budget efforts is unlikely to hold comparable views of the department head and the Chief Municipal Administrator.

Similarly, those who see themselves as receiving strong support from these administrative reviewers do not ordinarily expect much help from more expressly political bodies.

A projection of points onto Dimension II reflects a reality of alliance formation in municipal budgetary politics which is often beyond the control of the particular choices made by lower level officials: all agencies do not have access to or support from the governmental structures which they view as most influential in budgeting. If Dimension II is interpreted as an influence dimension, then the Chief Municipal Administrator, the department head, and the Council Finance Committee would appear to be the most influential elements. Of lesser but moderate influence are the Mayor, the Cabinet, and the City Council. The least influential element is apparently the layman political committees. It is natural that such a distinction is monitored in this set of support evaluations. Some agency officials have access to and are able to build alliances in budgeting with more influential governmental structures. Others must, as a reality of political life, rely upon the support of structures which they realize are less influential but, apparently, more accessible.

We have an unusual opportunity to provide validating evidence for the interpretation of a particular dimension drawn from the submission of data to a multidimensional scaling model. Too often, investigators must intuit the appropriate interpretation when, in fact, a number of other characterizations of a given dimension would be equally plausible. In Figure 1, the means were presented for evaluations of the level of influence exerted by each of these seven structures. These responses serve as an independent validating measure for the accuracy of the interpretation of Dimension II. The rank correlation between a projection of points into Dimension II and the mean levels of influence for each structure depicted in Figure 1 is, with the sole exception of the location of the mayor, perfect – an observation which strengthens the view that support from governmental structures of varying degrees of influence strongly shapes the patterns of alliances in municipal budgetary politics.

Alliance Structure Support and Budget Success

Agency officials develop views and expectations about the structures in government with which they must deal in budgeting. Some participating structures are seen as quite influential; others much less so. Some are viewed as competent to do budget work while others are not. The actual building of alliances with these alternative structures hinges on both individual choice and objective reality. Some agency officials appear willing to deal with structures composed of politicians and apparently gain much support from that effort; others seem to rely for budget support on familiar administrative elements. But, support is not solely a matter of choice. Some lower level officials are fortunate enough to benefit from the support of more influential elements in budgeting while others must rely upon the efforts of municipal bodies more peripheral to the budgetary process.

Yet, the central point in our analysis certainly has to do with the consequences of that support or opposition for budget success. Presumably agency officials cultivate the support of different governmental structures because they believe that such support affects the successes and failures of their efforts toward budget expansion. Those agencies which enjoy a high level of support from a number of these participating structures would be expected to fare quite well during the budget review process. Others, with more limited access and support, may suffer during that process as a result.

In terms comparable to the assessment of party politics and budget success, we may formalize these expectations about alliance structure politics and budget success:

$$S_{qi} = b_0 + \sum_{k=1}^{7} b_k y_{ki} + e_i$$

where

S_q = budgetary success with q=1, . . ., 9 according to the particular formulation of the dependent variable defined above.

y_{ki} = agency official i's evaluation of alliance element k's tendency to be on his side, on a scale from 0 to 10.

and the b_k's are regression parameters to be estimated.

Thus, we anticipate that budget success varies systematically with estimated support from different governmental structures which participate, formally or informally, in the budgetary process.

The results for each multiple regression analysis, consistent with the above formalization, are presented in Table 1. As was the case for party support and budget success in the preceding chapter, each measure of budgetary change is conceived of as a linear function of the level of support from these seven potential alliance elements. The entries in Table 1, however, do not support the view that the postures of these governmental structures toward particular agencies systematically affect the budget successes and failures of those agencies. For none of the

Table 1. Budgetary Change as Linear Functions of Support from Seven Alliance Elements

Dependent Variable	Squared Multiple Correlation Coefficients*
Level Specific Budget Change:	
dept rec/agen req	.102
CMA rec/dept rec	.240
Coun app/CMA rec	.164
Cumulative Budget Change:	
dept rec/agen req	.102
CMA rec/agen req	.221
Coun rec/agen req	.223
Appropriations Increase Budget Change:	
agen req/prior app	.181
dept rec/prior app	.173
CMA rec/prior app	.111
Coun app/prior app	.110

* No relationships statistically significant at .05 level; n ≅ 50.

Table 2. Budgetary Change as Linear Functions of Support from Two Bureaucratic Alliance Elements.

Dependent Variable	Squared Multiple Correlation Coefficient
Level Specific Budget Change:	
dept rec/agen req	.058
CMA rec/dept rec	.070
Coun app/CMA rec	.040
Cumulative Budget Change:	
dept rec/agen req	.058
CMA rec/agen req	.083
Coun rec/agen req	.032
Appropriations Increase Budget Change:	
agen req/prior app	.187*
dept rec/prior app	.172*
CMA rec/prior app	.166*
Coun app/prior app	.166*

* Statistically significant at .05 level; n ≅ 60

dependent variables are we able to account for a statistically significant proportion of the variance in budget success.

We referred earlier to customary formulations of this general problem in terms of the importance of bureaucratic politics for government decision-making. The elements of that argument, as we suggested above, may be treated as a subset of the general model which we have called the alliance structure model. The two of the seven potential alliance elements which are distinctly bureaucratic (the department head and the Chief Municipal Administrator) may be selected for a separate assessment of the consequences of their support for budget success. A restricted treatment of the importance of these two elements alone would not, of course, increment the proportion of variance explained in budget success by the full set of seven. We have, however, relied upon tests of statistical significance in these assessments. If the five expressly political alliance elements are, in fact, of trivial importance, then the degrees of freedom lost by the inclusion of these additional peripheral variables would diminish the statistical significance of the full assessment.

The entries in Table 2 provide some slight evidence that this may have happened in some cases. The measures of appropriations increase, when treated as linear functions of support from these two bureaucratic elements alone, achieve statistical significance; but the level of explanatory power is not great. Nonetheless, the measures of level-specific and cumulative budget success remain unrelated to the estimated level of support from these two principal bureaucratic elements.

Conclusions: The Politics of Budgeting

In this chapter and in the former chapter, we have tried to discuss the question of the validity of two alternative conceptions of politics and government decision. The party programmatic model of the politics of budgeting holds that controversies and conflicts over the issues of public spending take place among political parties and that the successes and failures of spending proposals are determined by the stances of those political parties. The alliance structure model, in contrast, posits a shift from political party to government structure. Conflicting orientations toward the issues of government spending characterize different structures in government; and the successes and failures of spending proposals devolve upon the support or opposition obtained from those structures. The entries in Table 3 provide a composite view of our findings on the relative importance of these two conceptions of the politics of budgeting. As the squared multiple partial correlation coefficients indicate, over one half of the variance in budget success can be accounted for by the political party support variables – even after the support of these particular government structures has been held constant. A control for the party support variables, however, renders even more trivial the independent contribution of the alliance structure variables.

We ought to give some attention to what it means to choose between these two particular models. We believe the issues to be clear in general terms: Is the politics of budgeting better understood as a process of conflict, compromise, support, opposition among political parties or among structures in government? But, in concrete terms, the issues of choice between the two models become confused as political parties come to be formally represented on several of these structures; and members of political parties utilize their positions of influence on these structures to pursue party goals. We realize also that these findings are at variance with those of other studies of budgeting. Finally, these results seem counter-intuitive – given what is often assumed about the

Table 3. Relative Explanatory Power of Political Party Support Variables and Alliance Structure Support Variables*

Dependent Variable	Variance Explained in Budget Change by:	
	Political Party Support, controlling for Alliance Structure Support	Alliance Structure Support, controlling for Political Party Support
Level-Specific Budget Change:		
dept rec/agen req	.616	.095
CMA rec/dept rec	.586	.238
Coun app/CMA rec	.554	.065
Cumulative Budget Change:		
dept rec/agen req	.616	.095
CMA rec/agen req	.639	.197
Coun rec/agen req	.570	.144
Appropriations Increase Budget Change:		
agen req/prior app	.614	.178
dept rec/prior app	.563	.170
CMA rec/prior app	.476	.183
Coun app/prior app	.525	.225

*$n \cong 35$.

declining importance of political parties and legislatures and the parallel increasing importance of civil servants and bureaucracies in the modern state. We want to address these broader issues in these concluding remarks.

In this vein, an important assumption of the alliance structure model deserves re-emphasis: Different structures in government are assumed to develop distinct orientations and views about the issues of public spending. The Chief Municipal Administrator is likely to be a 'budget cutter'. The City Council will probably restore depleted funds (much as the American Senate Appropriations Committee is assumed to do). The City Cabinet is likely to favor budget expansion. Implicit in that assumption is the view that developing orientations around structures in government mute the saliency of partisan controversies among members of those structures – at least for five of these seven structures on which parties are represented. Thus, distinct orientations become associated with different structures, despite their partisan composition. Presumably this is not a problem in the case of the two bureaucratic structures dealt with here.

It is this assumption of the alliance structure model which is probably least plausible. We would infer, though we cannot directly observe, that partisan controversies remain salient among members of these alternative political structures. Thus, it is not helpful to speak of distinct orientations for these different political structures toward issues of public spending; for the distinctiveness in orientation inheres in the parties, not in the structures on which they are represented. As a result, it is partisan orientation and controversy – albeit played out within different government structures – which best accounts for budgetary change from one year to the next.

This should not be taken to mean that these structures in government are unimportant for budgeting; they quite clearly are. Some of these structures are formally responsible for decisional outputs. Others provide the principal opportunities available to party members for influencing budgetary decisions. Still others retain staffs of experts which undoubtedly influence the direction of government spending. These data, however, support the view that the successes and failures for agencies on issues of budget expansion devolve upon the postures of the parties themselves – utilizing a variety of formal and informal mechanisms to shape the direction of government spending.

From this standpoint it is worth emphasizing that, in these various formulations of the dependent variable, we are not dealing with the concept of *base* but rather with the concept of *change* – the magnitude of change introduced by various reviewers in agency budget requests and the magnitude of change in appropriations increases from one year to the next. We have no doubt that, were we to focus solely on the concept of base, the importance of the two bureaucratic elements in the alliance structure model – the department head and the Chief Municipal Administrator – would mushroom; and the seven political parties would be relegated to a rather insignificant stance.

These findings provide little support for the inference that the budgetary process – the set of mechanisms by which societies go about allocating public financial resources – has become so isolated, bureaucratized, and self-perpetuating as to render political control over those decisions meaningless. It is not of trivial importance that changes in the direction of government spending seem closely tied to the postures of political parties. While we would not anticipate that parties propose to mass electorates vast and wide-ranging alterations in the nature of government activity (e.g., substantial changes in budget base), it is certainly plausible that the programs and platforms, proposed by political parties, necessitate marginal to moderate changes in the contents of budgets. One empirical manifestation of this is the tendency, which we have documented above, for changes in agency budget requests and changes in agency appropriations to covary with the estimated level of support of political parties for government agencies. We certainly cannot address, with these data, the broader question of the relationships between those actions and true mass preferences; but, the linkage between political parties and government activity has always constituted an important component of Western democratic theory. The relevance of these findings for the empirical validity of that linkage seems evident.

VI. Organizing for Budgeting: Agency Resources and Budget Change

We have dealt thus far with successively more proximate elements in the choice environments of public officials. The most distant of those elements were the policy environments of different agencies – the satisfactions and dissatisfactions of relevant publics and the demands and preferences of organized pressure groups. These elements are most distant from budgeting in the sense that they are external to the individual agencies, to other government institutions, and to the party system. Second, and somewhat more proximate, were the political parties – more proximate from the standpoint of their formal representation on structures which participate in budgeting. Third, and more directly linked to the budgetary process, are the various government structures with which agencies must deal directly in budgeting. We have omitted, however, considerations of factors which inhere in particular characteristics of government agencies themselves; and we wish to redress that omission in this chapter by treating the relevance of those properties, internal to lower-level governmental units, for budgetary politics and budgetary change.

Agency budget requests are not solely at the mercies of reviewers. Any governmental unit will have at its disposal a set of resources generated by the formal establishment of that unit. We shall consider two kinds of organizational resources, held by these agencies, which may facilitate or retard budget expansion. As in virtually every other kind of decision-making setting, budgets are influenced by some factors over which decision-makers have direct control and by others which are beyond the bounds of human choice. Resources of the first kind may be manipulated by government agencies in order to maximize goal attainment. Resources of the second kind – although their presence or absence may distinguish quite sharply those who succeed and those who fail – are not manipulated by organizations and decision-makers who retain them.

Manipulatable Resources and Budget Change

Organizations rarely remain completely powerless in the face of adversity. Most organizations will come to possess, over a period of time, a number of potent resources which may be manipulated to their advantage in times of organizational stress. From a budgeting perspective, the meaning of organizational stress is self-evident: It is budget failure – failure in obtaining requested increases for the upcoming fiscal year. The most manipulatable of resources for agency chiefs are the individuals who work under them; and it is natural that, during times of budget failure, agency officials turn to those who may have had a significant input into agency budget decisions in the past.

We shall consider in this section two conventional organizational responses to stress situations of this kind. Each represents a way in which agency officials allocate and re-allocate personnel time to budgeting under conditions of past budget failure. First, we examine the determinants and consequences of the frequency of budget meetings – both within the agency and between the agency and external influentials. Second, we focus on the specific allocation of agency personnel to budget preparation work. Each of these manipulatable responses is conceived of as a function of prior budget failures.

Changes in organizational behavior necessarily involve changes in the behavior of personnel. If an official wishes that his agency engage in some activity which it has not engaged in before or that his agency give more attention to one kind of activity than to others, then he will naturally be led to changes in the allocation of personnel time for various activities. The myriad of studies in government which attempt to estimate the amount of time spent on various tasks reflect that underlying assumption. But the dynamics and the consequences of personnel change are never self-evident in situations of this kind. What kinds of conditions stimulate change and what are the consequences of those changes? We hope to provide some partial answers to these questions in this section – at least as regards agency personnel and budget work in the Oslo municipal government.

Those of us who have spent time in organizations of various kinds have, no doubt, spent a goodly portion of that time in meetings. Particularly during the period of budget preparation and review, higher level agency officials and reviewing agents spend no trivial amount of time discussing budget issues – accuracy of estimates and forecasts, equipment and supply needs of various offices, political palatability of request levels, etc. Such meetings may serve various functions for the organization – consensus building, information distribution, strategy mapping, and so forth. At a minimum, however, the practice of holding formal meetings on conflictual issues is indicative of one way in which agency officials manipulate internal resources – personnel time – as they respond to conditions of stress.

It is useful to think of these kinds of organizational responses to stress in process terms – particularly, the antecedents of response (budget failure), the kind of response (increase in frequency of agency budget meetings), and the consequences of that response (budget success). Our access to cross-sectional data with series budget entries allows us to treat this kind of problem with somewhat greater precision. We define organizational stress for the specific case of budgeting as the percentage of the agency's budget request actually approved in the preceding year. Two time periods are relevant here. First, budget failures in the preceding year may stimulate the holding of budget meetings in the current year in order to insure that past failures are not repeated. Second, the frequency of budget meetings in the current year may increase as a function of budget failures at preceding levels during the current budget review process. For example, severe deletions from agency budgets by the Chief Municipal Administrator may encourage agency meetings with members of the City Council in an effort to have those funds restored. Thus, we are able to treat both long-term and short-term conceptions of budget stress.

We have asked these agency officials to tell us something of the frequency of such budget meetings during the period immediately preceding the submission of budget requests to higher level reviewing agents and during the period of budget review.[1] We suspect that, during this period of budget preparation, the frequency of meetings within the agency, with other bureaucratic participants, and with more expressly political participants increases; and we hypothesize, first, that this frequency is a negative function of budget success in the preceding year.

That hypothesis is born out in part by the entries in Table 1. Budget failures in the preceding year stimulate meetings between agency personnel and various *political* bodies in the municipality – the Mayor, the layman political committees, and the City Council. Indeed, the correlation between overall budget success in the preceding year and the frequency of agency meetings with the City Council during current budget deliberations is a substantial -.702. Budget failures, however, do not appear to encourage budget meetings among bureaucratic participants – either within the agency or between the agency and the department head or the Chief Municipal Administrator. Apparently, political bodies are viewed as the more potent contact points for agencies which have suffered budget failures in the past; and civil servants in these agencies spend significantly more time in meetings with these political bodies when their past budget efforts have been less than successful.

It is likely, however, that agency officials will try to have their say in budget meetings with reviewing agents as they experience difficulties during current budget deliberations as well. But this kind of problem requires consideration in more expressly process terms. Our expectation here is that the frequency of agency budget meetings with a given reviewing agent (an indication of the amount of time spent by personnel in budget meetings) will increase as a negative function of budget success at the preceding stage of review. From this perspective we may formulate a path analytic model which incorporates both long-term and

Table 1. Relationships between Budget Success in Preceding Year (1973) and Frequency of Budget Meetings with Different Municipal Structures in Current Year (1974): Pearson Product-Moment Correlation Coefficients.

Budget Success in Preceding Year (1973):	Frequency of Budget Meetings in Current Year with:					
	own agency personnel	dept head	Chf Mun Adm	Mayor	layman pol com	Council
Level-Specific Budget Change						
dept rec/agen req	.091	-.062	-.050	-.223	-.189	-.335*
CMA rec/dept rec	-.171	.027	.059	-.063	-.069	-.221
Coun app/CMA rec	.020	.185	.098	.088	.171	.126
Cumulative Budget Change						
dept rec/agen req	.091	-.062	-.050	-.223	-.189	-.335*
CMA rec/agen req	-.063	-.046	.013	-.391*	-.327*	-.702*
Coun app/agen req	-.062	-.020	.029	-.389*	-.309*	-.702*

* Statistically significant at .05 level; n ≅ 67.

short-term conceptions of budget failure. We define the following quantities:

X_1: 1973 Budget Success (percentage of agency request appropriated by City Council)

X_2: R's estimate of frequency of budget meetings within own agency during 1974 budget preparation and review

X_3: Agency Budget Acquisitiveness (1974 agency request as a percentage of 1973 Council appropriation)

X_4: R's estimate of frequency of agency budget meetings with department head during 1974 budget preparation and review

X_5: 1974 recommendation by department head for the agency as a percentage of agency request

X_6: R's estimate of frequency of agency budget meetings with Chief Municipal Administrator during 1974 budget preparation and review

X_7: 1974 recommendation by Chief Municipal Administrator for the agency as a percentage of departmental recommendation for the agency

X_8: R's estimate of frequency of agency budget meetings with members of City Council during 1974 budget preparation and review

X_9: 1974 appropriation by the City Council for the agency as a percentage of recommendation by the Chief Municipal Administrator for the agency.

Our expectations may now be formalized in process terms:

$$X_2 = p_{21}X_1 + e_2$$
$$X_3 = p_{31}X_1 + p_{32}X_2 + e_3$$
$$X_4 = p_{41}X_1 + p_{43}X_3 + e_4$$
$$X_5 = p_{51}X_1 + p_{53}X_3 + p_{54}X_4 + e_5$$
$$X_6 = p_{61}X_1 + p_{65}X_5 + e_6$$
$$X_7 = p_{71}X_1 + p_{73}X_3 + p_{75}X_5 + p_{76}X_6 + e_7$$
$$X_8 = p_{81}X_1 + p_{87}X_7 + e_8$$
$$X_9 = p_{91}X_1 + p_{93}X_3 + p_{95}X_5 + p_{98}X_8 + e_9$$

There are several elements to the process which we wish to model with these equations. First, the frequency of budget meetings between the agency and a given reviewing agent is a function of (1) overall budget success in the preceding year and (2) budget success at the review stage immediately prior to the one in question for the current year's deliberations (Equations for X_2, X_4, X_6, X_8). Failures during either of those time periods are expected to increase the frequency of budget meetings within the agency and with reviewing agents as a means of lessening the probability of such failures during subsequent budget deliberations.

Second, we wish to know whether the frequency of meetings on budget issues holds much consequence for subsequent budget successes or failures (Equations for X_3, X_5, X_7, X_9). Do those agency officials who establish a pattern of holding meetings between their staffs and higher level reviewers fare much better in budget deliberations? Alternative hypotheses here postulate that budget successes or failures are simply repetitive from one year to the next or from one stage to the next; and that the effects of conscious efforts to alter those established patterns of behavior are negligible.

These expectations are represented in the form of a path diagram in

Figure 1. Since these equations are recursive, ordinary least-squares solutions are appropriate; those estimates are entered on the diagram in Figure 1.[2] These results support our initial observations based upon the correlation coefficients in Table 1. In no case are we able to account for the frequency of agency meetings on budget issues with bureaucratic reviewers. Neither budget failures in the preceding year nor budget failures at specific levels in the current year appear to stimulate more frequent formal contacts between agency personnel and the department head or the Chief Municipal Administrator.

Figure 1

Path Diagram: Prior Budget Success, Meetings with Municipal Decision Makers, and Current Budgetary Consequences

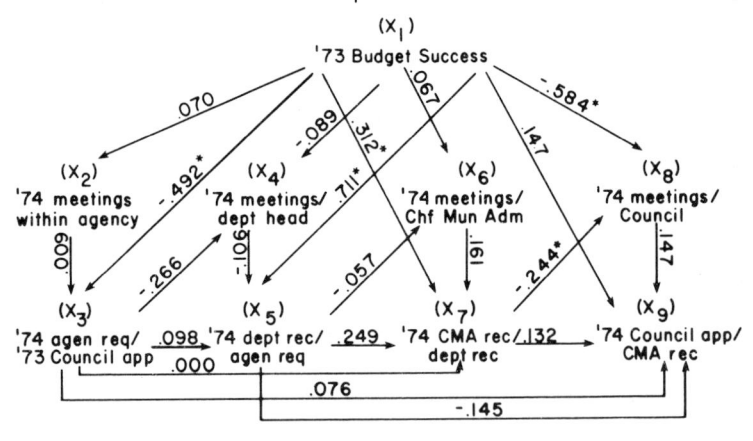

(X_1) '73 Budget Success

(X_2) '74 meetings within agency
(X_4) '74 meetings/ dept head
(X_6) '74 meetings/ Chf Mun Adm
(X_8) '74 meetings/ Council

(X_3) '74 agen req/ '73 Council app
(X_5) '74 dept rec/ agen req
(X_7) '74 CMA rec/ dept rec
(X_9) '74 Council app/ CMA rec

.070, .089, .312*, .067, .147, -.584*, .492*, .711*, -.266, -.106, -.057, -.244*, .098, .000, .249, .132, .147, .191, .076, -.145

*Significant at .05 level

Formal contact through meetings with members of the City Council, however, is another matter indeed. Those agencies who have suffered during the budget deliberations of the preceding year or who have been treated severely by the Chief Municipal Administrator's office in the current year are significantly more likely to seek contact through meetings with municipal Council members (p_{81} = -.584; p_{87} = -.244). Budget stress situations of this kind apparently encourage conventional organizational responses in which agency personnel spend significantly more time in formal meetings; but the focus of those contacts through meetings is on expressly political bodies.

The consequences (in terms of budget change) of frequent agency meetings with any of these reviewing levels are, however, negligible. The strongest predictor of budget acquisitiveness and budget success remains the past experiences of the agency. We should not make too much of that conclusion; for, as our analyses in earlier chapters bear out, important explanatory variables are omitted from the path analytic model in Figure 1. Nonetheless, it is fair to say that budget success for these agencies appears unrelated to the frequency of agency meetings with various reviewing agents on budget issues – a point to which we shall return below.

A second, and perhaps more direct, response to past budget failures may be observed in the specific allocation of higher level personnel to budget preparation work. There is considerable variability across these agencies on the dispersion of budget work among agency personnel. For some, budget preparation is the nearly exclusive domain of the agency chief and financial officer. Others bring additional personnel into the request formulation process on a part-time basis. In some of these agencies, several higher level officials devote their full attention to budget preparation during the several weeks preceding the submission of requests. Our expectation here – from a perspective comparable to that for our analysis of the frequency of formal meetings on budget issues – is that the allocation of personnel to budget preparation work varies inversely with prior budget successes.

Agency officials were asked during the interview to estimate the numbers of higher level employees devoted full time to budget work and part-time to budget work in the period immediately preceding the submission of requests. We also obtained estimates of the total number of higher level employees in the agency. These three estimates provide a basis for deriving an index of relative budget effort for each agency:

$$\text{Relative Budget Effort} = \frac{n_f + (n_p/2)}{n_t}$$

where:

n_f = number of agency officials devoted full time to budget work
n_p = number of agency officials devoted part-time to budget work
n_t = total number of higher level agency officials.

Thus, we assume that an official who devotes only part of his time to budget preparation work represents only one-half as much budget effort for the agency as would the official who spends nearly all of his time on budget work during this period. Since the number of officials may vary a good deal from agency to agency, we correct for size in order to produce a measure of relative budget effort.

The correlation coefficients in Table 2 support the hypothesis that prior budget failures stimulate officials to allocate more personnel time to current budget work. Particularly for the measure of overall budget success in the preceding year (1973 Council appropriation as a percentage of agency request), the correlation estimate of -0.474 is sizeable. Thus, the less successful an agency is in obtaining requested budget increases in the preceding year, the greater the relative allocation of personnel to budget work in the following year.

Table 2. Relationships between Relative Allocation of Personnel to Budget Work and Budget Success in 1973
(Pearson Product-Moment Correlation Coefficients)

	1973
Level-Specific Success	
dept rec/agen req	-.269*
CMA rec/dept rec	-.043
Coun app/CMA rec	-.176
Cumulative Success	
dept rec/agen req	-.269*
CMA rec/agen req	-.433*
Coun rec/agen req	-.474*

* Statistically significant at .05 level; n = 52.

Presumably, however, relationships of this magnitude reflect the underlying judgments of officials that such actions are effective, that they hold consequences for budget successes and failures in following time periods. Again in process terms, we may formulate a path analytic model which indicates the validity of that assumption. We define the following qualities:

X_1 = 1973 Budget Success (percentage of agency request appropriated by City Council)

X_2 = Relative Budget Effort

X_3 = Agency Budget Acquisitiveness (1974 agency request as a percentage of 1973 Council appropriation)

X_4 = 1973 recommendation by department head for the agency as a percentage of agency request

X_5 = 1974 recommendation by Chief Municipal Administrator for the agency as a percentage of departmental recommendation for the agency

X_6 = 1974 appropriation by the City Council for the agency as a percentage of recommendation by the Chief Municipal Administrator for the agency.

and the following set of structural equations:

$X_2 = p_{21}X_1 + e_2$
$X_3 = p_{31}X_1 + p_{32}X_2 + e_3$
$X_4 = p_{41}X_1 + p_{42}X_2 + p_{43}X_3 + e_4$
$X_5 = p_{51}X_1 + p_{52}X_2 + p_{53}X_3 + p_{54}X_4 + e_5$
$X_6 = p_{61}X_1 + p_{62}X_2 + p_{63}X_3 + p_{64}X_4 + p_{65}X_5 + e_6$

The first equation (X_2) postulates that relative budget effort in one year is a function of budget successes or failures in the previous year. Remaining equations (X_3, X_4, X_5, X_6) formalize our expectation that budgetary acquisitiveness and success at each stage is a function of (1) budget successes and failures in the previous year, (2) relative budget effort, and (3) actions taken at preceding levels during the current year's budget formulation and review process.

Ordinary least-squares estimates for the path coefficients are recorded on the diagram in Figure 2. Our conclusions from those estimates closely parallel those for the frequency of budget meetings:

Figure 2

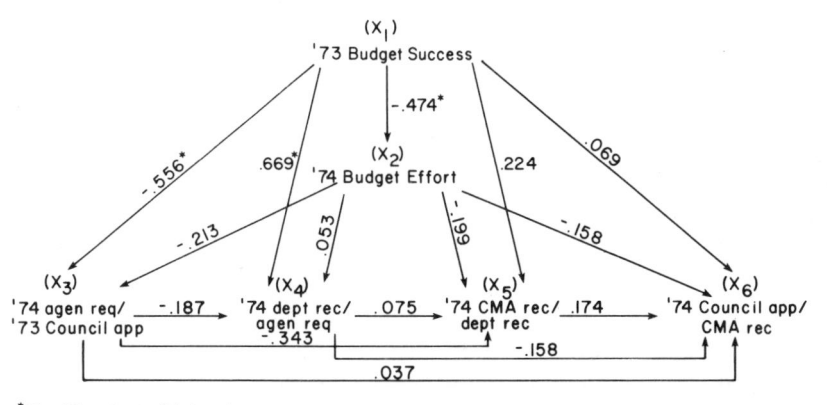

Prior Budget Success, Relative Budget Effort and Current Budgetary Consequences

*Significant at .05 level

negative budget experiences in the previous year encourage officials to reallocate internal resources for goal attainment (budget success) in the following year; but those reallocations have little independent effect on budget success. At no decision point in the 1974 decisions did relative budget effort show any independent effect on budget change.

We have been able to account rather well for changes in the allocation of internal agency resources – in this case, personnel – by conceiving of those allocations as functions of prior failures in goal attainment. Specifically, failures in obtaining requested increases in preceding years stimulate agency officials to use relatively more personnel (1) in frequent meetings on budget issues with elected politicians and (2) in specific budget preparation work – presumably in efforts to insure that past failures are not repeated during current review processes. Our ability to account for the causes underlying the changes in personnel resource allocation, however, stands in marked contrast to our ability to demonstrate any systematic effect of those variations on actual agency budget acquisitiveness or budget success during the subsequent time period. While these actions may be seen by agency officials as natural responses to prior budget failures, their effects on current budget successes and failures appear negligible.

These patterns–systematic responses to failures in goal attainment without demonstrable effects of those responses – naturally raise questions about the persistence of those practices over time. If officials learn from experience, as they presumably do, then the strength of the relationship between prior budget failures and the manipulation of these internal resources should diminish over time. Yet, we do not expect, in the real world of budgeting, that this is so; for such a decision-making scenario assumes that officials are able to gauge, systematically, the consequences of their actions.

Budget successes and failures are rarely self-evident to decision-makers who experience them. Since budgets are almost never accepted or rejected in total, but rather, are approved in part, dichotomous judgments about success or failure are difficult. As a result, decision-makers can rarely say that goals (budget success) have been attained or not; they have, in contrast, been more or less approximated. We do not mean to say that decision-makers do not hold reasonably accurate perceptions about their relative degrees of success; they certainly do. But is, for example, a ninety-five percent funding of an agency budget request indicative of budget success or budget failure? As long as the lines are not clearly drawn for such judgments, we believe that officials will continue to take action designed to improve budget success over preceding years – although they may be unable to gauge systematically the consequences of those actions.

We suspect, also, that a second condition of decision-making in government – the multiplicity of factors influencing choice – lessens the utility of learning models in accounting for actions of government officials. As long as decision-makers are aware that several factors influence their successes and failures at higher levels of budget review, their ability to gauge the potency of any one action will be diminished. For example, an agency official may decide to devote a substantial number of personnel to budget work in order to prepare more careful estimates and to improve his chances for success. But, if he continues to be treated severely by reviewing agents, does he conclude that such personnel reallocations are trivial; or does he attribute those failures to any of several other factors? As the decision-making setting becomes more complex, the ability of decision-makers to assess accurately the effects of particular actions on outcomes diminishes. As a result, certain choices and actions, which appear to be rational for goal maximization, may continue to be taken – although their systematic consequences may be negligible.

Nonmanipulatable Resources and Budget Change

While some organizational resources are subject to manipulation and change, others are more constant and enduring features of the landscape. They are constant in the sense that, although they may distinguish sharply those who succeed and those who fail, they cannot be manipulated to facilitate success or to impede failure. Thus, they stand in sharp contrast to those factors we considered in the preceding section. Many of the customary variables of aggregate policy studies are of this generic type. Personal income in societies as a determinant of government spending is perhaps the best example. Subnational governmental units cannot manipulate the level of income in their jurisdictions, although that level of income remains a strong determinant of financial resources available to those governmental units for public spending. We shall consider three kinds of relatively stationary properties which set some of these administrative units apart from others – properties which would seem to provide a natural advantage for some during the budgeting exercise: (1) the presence of a planning unit within the organizational structure; (2) the size of the agency, both in terms of personnel and budget; and (3) the restrictions placed upon its spending options by the Norwegian central government.

Roughly one-half ot these agencies retain their own planning units. Two of the most important functions of these planning units are (1) the carrying out of careful studies of particular problems faced by the agency, and (2) the formulation of plans of implementation for new policy proposals. The effects of these activities may be felt in at least two ways during annual budget deliberations. First, the stimulative effect on budget expansion efforts may be considerable. The presence of a planning unit in an agency may be viewed as evidence of institutionalized innovation. New spending proposals may be forthcoming at a much higher rate if administrative units are organized in such a way that specific subunits have responsibility for analyzing problems and proposing new solutions. Second, the appending of concrete plans and research reports to budget requests may help to insure more favorable budget treatment by reviewers. As such, the planning office may constitute one of the more important internal organizational resources of the agency on matters subject to budgetary review.

Means for each of the measures of budget change are shown in Figure 3 for two groups of agency officials: (A) those whose agencies have a planning unit and (B) those whose agencies have no planning unit. For the first two conceptions of budget change (level-specific budget change and cumulative change), the findings are consistently in contrast to our expectations: budget requests from agencies with no planning unit are treated more favorably by reviewers than are those from agencies with their own planning units. These findings are made more explicable, however, by an examination of the third graph in Figure 3. Those agencies with planning units are simply more acquisitive in budget request formulations than are those without such units and, in terms of final appropriations increases from one year to the next, remain the more successful.

The means in these graphs resurrect the pattern of paradoxes evident in our analysis of clientele effects on budget change in Chapter III. Recall that those agencies with large concentrations of dissatisfied clientele were actually treated the most severely during the review of budget requests; yet, those same agencies were the most successful in obtaining appropriations increases. The same pattern is evident in our analysis of planning unit effects; and we interpret it in terms of the same institutionalized response mechanisms. The principal effect of planning units within agencies lies in their stimulative impact on budget acquisitiveness; requested budget increases by agency officials who held their own planning units exceeded requested increases for those who did not by more than five percent. Reviewers, responding to a different set of concerns, view budget acquisitiveness in any form with some suspicion. Thus, in terms of level-specific and cumulative budget change, those agencies with planning units suffer relatively greater losses – a result, however, of their heightened acquisitiveness. Nonetheless, that acquisitiveness apparently has payoffs in the long run. From the standpoint of actual appropriations increases, they remain the more

Figure 3

Presence of Planning Office within Agency and Budget Change

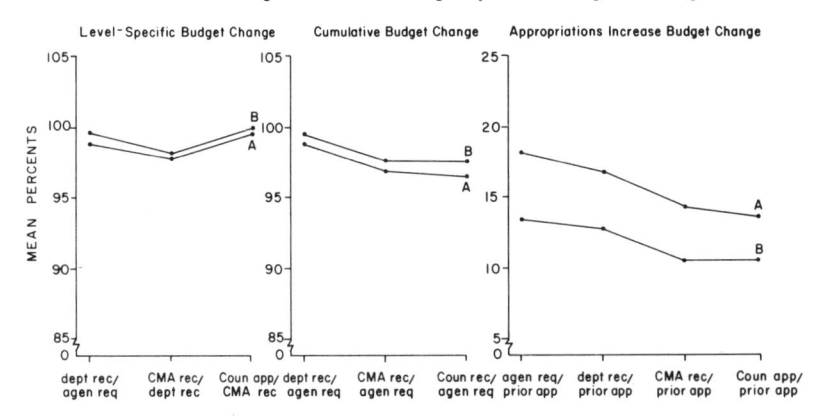

[Figure showing three graphs: Level-Specific Budget Change, Cumulative Budget Change, and Appropriations Increase Budget Change, with mean percents on y-axis.

KEY: A. Planning Office within Agency; n = 38.
B. No Planning Office within Agency; n = 32.]

successful – even though intermediate cuts are more severe.

A second, relatively stable property of individual agencies which may have some impact on their successes and failures in budgeting is the size of the agency. While we are only beginning to understand the consequences of some of these organizational conditions for budgeting, some earlier work leads us to expect a negative impact of agency size on budget success. Barber, in his experimental study of budgeting by local financial decision-makers in New England, found that, when budget cuts are to be made, attention is naturally drawn to large items in agency budgets.[3] Extrapolating from these findings from item to total agency budgets, we would expect the more severe cuts by reviewers to be concentrated in the budgets of larger agencies. We would expect the opposite pattern, however, if it is true that the larger agencies possess more political 'muscle' and, by virtue of that, receive more favorable treatment from reviewers.

Size, with respect to administrative units, seems to mean at least two somewhat different things. First, the number of employees (civil servants) taps one dimension of what we ordinarily mean by agency size. Second, the magnitude of the agency budget (in this case, the 1973 budget) may serve as an additional measure of agency size. The relationships between these two indicators of size and budget change are shown in Table 3. There is no indication that a large number of civil servants has any impact on agency successes and failures in budgeting. None of these relationships is statistically significant.

Table 3. Relationships between Agency Size and Budget Change (Pearson Product-Moment Correlation Coefficients)

	Agency Size	
	number of employees	1973 Budget Allocation
Level-Specific Budget Change		
dept rec/agen req	.028	.215*
CMA rec/dept rec	-.008	.006
Coun app/CMA rec	-.036	-.466*
Cumulative Budget Change		
dept rec/agen req	.028	.215*
CMA rec/agen req	.004	.091
Coun rec/agen req	-.012	-.120
Appropriations Increase Budget Change		
Agen req/prior app	.056	-.278*
dept rec/prior app	.063	-.263*
CMA rec/prior app	.068	-.261*
Coun app/prior app	.063	-.280*
	n = 61	n = 83

* Statistically significant at .05 level.

The effects of size, as reflected in the magnitude of agency budgets, appear to be more systematic. With respect to budget change at specific levels in the review process, larger agencies are treated slightly more favorably by departmental reviewers while smaller agencies are treated substantially more favorably by the City Council. Furthermore, for appropriations increase budget change, the smaller agencies appear to be slightly more acquisitive and slightly more successful in obtaining those increases. Thus, we cannot argue, in general, that the present size of an agency has much of an effect on its successes and failures in budgeting. We do find slight but consistent negative relationships, with respect to both appropriations increases at each stage of review and action on government-proposed budgets at the stage of Council review. There may be some tendency, of moderate strength, to treat smaller agencies more kindly.

A final stationary property of these agencies, likely to affect budgeting and spending, is the extent of flexibility available to them in implementing new programs and activities and dropping old ones. It is a fact of life for many of these agencies that what they do is externally determined – by the laws, policies, and programs of the Norwegian central government. For some, a substantial proportion of their budget allocations is fixed; and, their flexibility for innovation and change is much reduced as a result. Our respondents were asked during the interview to estimate the percentage of their budgets which was bound by national law or policy. These percentage estimates range from near zero to nearly 100 percent.

Our expectations regarding the effects of these national restrictions on budget change vary, depending on the particular formulation of the dependent variable. First, we expect a negative effect on budget acquisitiveness. Some of our respondents indicated, on occasion, that such restrictions limited the time and effort they could devote to more innovative proposals; and they seemed to resent those limitations. Thus, we hypothesize that those agencies which are free of such bounds will respond more freely to local needs and demands, and that the results will appear in the form of more expansive budgets for those units.

Action at specific reviewing levels is another matter. When the policies of the central government are such that local governments are

Table 4. Type of Interest Group Contact with Agency*

	(a) Percent	(N)
continuous contact	66.1%	(39)
sporadic contact	30.5	(18)
both	3.4	(2)
	(b) Percent	(N)
existing activities	63.2%	(36)
new activities	24.6	(14)
both	12.3	(7)
	(c) Percent	(N)
expenditure questions	17.9%	(10)
substantive policy questions	67.9	(38)
both	14.3	(8)

* Question wording (forced choice): We are interested in the kind of contact your agency has with these organizations. (a) Would you say that such contact is continuous throughout the year or is it only sporadic or occasional? (b) Does that contact usually concern the proposing of new activities for your agency, or are these organizations primarily concerned with how you carry out your current activities? (c) Does that contact usually concern questions of spending (e.g. the adequacy of funding for various programs), or does it more frequently concern sustantive questions of policy or program?

required to do certain things, local budget reviewers are limited in their ability to reduce dramatically or to delete items from certain agency budgets. Furthermore, if we assume that the total municipal budget must be reduced by a certain amount, those cuts must be concentrated in the budgets of local agencies which are most free from national government policy restrictions. Thus, with respect to level-specific budget change, two decision criteria serve to differentiate those agencies which operate under severe national government restrictions from those which operate under relatively free conditions. The budgets of the former cannot be reduced so dramatically; and, as a consequence, proposed cuts must be disproportionately made up for in the budget proposals of more freely operating agencies.

These expectations are not supported by the entries in Table 4. None of the relationships between the estimate of the budget percent bound by national law and budget change is significant. At least at the level of individual agencies, national government restrictions seem to be neither a hindrance nor a help in local budget deliberations. It is likely, of course, that the relationships would be much stronger – were we dealing with individual agency programs.

Conclusions

The multiplicity of factors within organizations which affect decisions and behavior certainly exceeds the smattering of variables treated in this chapter. We have tried, however, to identify those factors which would be expected to affect specifically decisions on budgets and which would be expected to operate systematically across all administrative units. We have identified several sources of internal organizational strength which may facilitate or retard budget change – some of which may be manipulated for goal maximization by the decision-makers who retain them, others of which serve as properties of organizations which simply distinguish those who succeed from those who fail.

When they experience failures in obtaining requested budget increases in previous time periods, officials do manipulate internal resources available to them in efforts to improve their budget success scores in later time periods. Specifically, those agency officials whose budgets fared poorly during the 1973 deliberations did not hesitate to allocate relatively greater personnel effort to budgeting in the following year – both in terms of formal meetings with reviewers and in terms of actual work on budget documents. The former response was restricted to personnel meetings with political rather than bureaucratic elements. In neither instance, however, were there systematic effects of these responses on current budget success rates.

Similarly, the more stable properties of organizations – the presence of planning units, agency size, and central government budget restrictions – do not exhibit pervasive effects on budget change. Planning units within agencies operate primarily as a stimulant to budget acquisitiveness but matter very little in subsequent review decisions. The larger agencies (in terms of personnel) do not hold an advantage over smaller ones on matters of budgeting; the larger agencies (in terms of budget size), are, indeed, at a slight disadvantage. And, the extent to which these agencies' budgets are restrained by provisions of national law seems not to affect their successes or failures in local budgeting.

As we juxtapose the findings of this chapter alongside those of earlier chapters, we begin to develop a view of budgeting which is at variance with earlier studies – particularly those studies which view the budgeting exercise as an event largely isolated and insulated from external pressures. The significance of our findings on the effects of clientele judgments, pressure groups, and political parties seems to dwarf the significance of our evidence on internal agency effects. The sources of budget change seem less rooted in the particular characteristics or properties of individual administrative units and more in the general environmental, social, and political conditions which surround them. We confront this issue head-on in the final chapter.

VII. Studying Budgeting Historically: Decision Rule Analysis

Investigators who ask comparable questions of different kinds of data are often dismayed at inconsistencies in results. Correlations based on figures for aggregate units are not the same as those for disaggregated units. Cross-sectional relationships are rarely of the same magnitude as overtime relationships – even when the variables are the same. We are confronted with the potential for these difficulties as we lengthen the time span in this analysis. But, we believe it necessary to confront some of the questions raised with systematic observations obtained over a much longer period of time. Indeed, much of what participants do in budgeting is learned from repeated imersions in the budgeting exercise during several years preceding.

As we extend the time span of analysis, we shall make use of systematic time series data – agency request, departmental recommendation, Chief Municipal Administrator's recommendation, Council appropriation – for each agency over a nineteen-year period, 1953 to 1971. We have been tempted, on occasion, to ask to what extent these time series analyses support specific conclusions drawn from the cross-sectional analyses of previous chapters. Yet, our analysis strategy has not been tailored to that end. We soon discovered that specific hypotheses are more adequately tested with one kind of data or another – but rarely with both. Thus, our perspective in this chapter is the following: we have not sought to test the same hypotheses in preceding chapters with different kinds of data; but, rather, we ask different questions of these data – questions to which they seem more suited than do the cross-sectional data above. In the final chapter, however, an attempt is made to draw the two together – to assess the extent to which both have supported or discounted more general interpretations of the politics of budgeting in Oslo.

The underlying concept which links our cross-sectional analysis to our time series analysis of the politics of budgeting is that of strategy – 'the links between the goals of the agencies and their perceptions of the kinds of actions which will be effective in their political environment.'[1]

The evidence thus far indicates that those agencies which have cultivated the support of interest groups and political parties are likely to fare much better during the budget review process at one point in time. Yet, we can hardly argue that such strategies are set and dissolved from one year to the next. Rather, they undoubtedly reflect the cumulative experiences of a lifetime of conflict and compromise, trial and error, effort and disappointment. Furthermore, they are likely to achieve some stability over the years as reciprocal expectations develop among participants. Agencies come to expect certain actions from reviewers; and reviewers come to expect certain actions from agencies. The result is an intricate network of strategy, conflict, compromise, calculation, and guesswork which retains significant stable properties over an extended period of time.

It is no accident that we have avoided explicit statements about the precise content and form of these strategies and the kinds of calculations which are made. Although we asked our respondents to tell us something of the kinds of strategies they and others might have followed in budgeting, we were not convinced in hearing and reading these comments that they were sufficiently rich in detail. It seemed, rather, that there were better ways than the interview/questionnaire method to pursue the notion of strategy. Particularly, we wanted a method which (1) would not leave us at the mercies of our respondents on an enormously sensitive question; and (2) would allow an assessment of strategic calculations overtime.

Davis, Dempster, and Wildavsky, building upon Wildavsky's earlier work, have proposed and tested a set of linear decision rules which describe various strategies chosen by participants in the budgetary process for the American national government.[2] We have found that formulation particularly appealing from the standpoint of the interplay between description, formalization, and interpretation. A given strategy may be followed by an agency official in preparing his budget request for the coming fiscal year. That strategy may be described in purely verbal terms and subsequently modeled in the form of linear equations. The parameter estimates will typically have a straightforward interpretation, since (a) each variable in the decision rule equations is tied to a particular property of the strategy itself, and (b) the regression is carried out through the origin in order to insure a percentage interpretation.

By estimating the parameters of various simple and complex linear decision models, we shall attempt to arrive at a best-fitting equation for each agency at each level in the budgetary process – an equation which we believe best describes the strategic behavior of the agency or its appropriate reviewing agent over the nineteen-year period. Yet, it is fair to say that our long-term interests lie in the policy implications of strategic behavior. In this regard, the hypothesis that the strategies pursued by individual agencies and their reviewing agents will have implications for actual growth rates of expenditures for agency activities – quite apart from steering attempts by the government itself – is particularly intriguing. Thus, we shall examine the relationships between the acquisitiveness and the complexity of the strategy and the long-term growth rate of the agency, taking some care in dissecting the success or failure of intermediate reviewing levels in stemming the successes of particularly expansive agencies. In a final section of this chapter, we return to some of the initial cognitive assumptions of the models; and we utilize our set of systematic interview materials to examine the validity of those assumptions.

Expenditures for the municipal government of Oslo during the immediate postwar period were, of course, affected by the postwar rebuilding program of the national government.[3] Restrictions in the economic sector persisted from 1945 to 1949. By 1952 the transition from a war economy to a peace economy had ended with very few residual restrictions left on communal expenditure policy. The effect of the relaxation in 1952 of national governmental restrictions on communal investment policy is evident in the accelerated growth rate of communal expenditures – exceeding the growth rates of both national governmental expenditures and the gross national product. It is this post-1952 period on which we shall focus the present analysis.

Theoretical Decision Models

Multiple cues are parts of the decision history of both individuals and organizations. Few decisions can be adequately accounted for by conceiving of a decision as a function of one event, of one condition, of one piece of information, or whatever. Complexities may abound in what seems to be the simplest of decisional settings. Yet, the modeling of such real-world events becomes manifestly inefficient as the analyst attempts to envelop the totality. A department head may happen to become ill during the crucial time of legislative budgetary review, but the explicit inclusion in a model of such a stochastic factor would merely improve prediction, not explanation. Such stochastic factors aside, however, any number of alternative conditions, decisions, and expectations may guide a given decision. The models which we develop in this section contain only such elements as are generated by the internal bureaucratic mechanisms of the administrative/legislative budgetary apparatus itself.

A budgetary decision on how much to request, how much to recommend, or how much to appropriate for a given agency depends on a set of internal cues which may be arrayed along a temporal dimension. The simplest type of decisional style is characterized by a restricted reaction to the conditions or events of the current budgetary period. For example, the Chief Municipal Administrator may follow a rather simple decision rule by granting a fixed mean percentage of the department head's recommendation for a given agency. Such behavior is quite simple from the standpoint of both the number of elements considered and their temporal accessibility. There is only one quantity on which the decision is based; and that quantity is immediately available, since it was generated during the current budgetary period at the step immediately prior to the one in question. As a result, no search is required for information concerning the decision history of the agency, nor is it necessary to calculate future consequences of the decision. This simplest notion of process incrementalism is represented by the decision rules displayed in Table 1a.[4] The decision taken at a given stage during the budgetary proceedings is a function of the decision taken at the stage immediately before. Neither past relationships between the agency and its reviewing agents nor future expectations enter the calculus.

It is, of course, likely that the history of the system is quite relevant. We should make a distinction, however, based upon the temporal distance of such events. Any decision rule which postulates a reaction to an event occurring in the present year's budgetary period does not, of course, probe far into the history of the system. We interpret those decision rules as reactions primarily to the present, with some attention given to the short-term history of the decision. The decision rules set out in Table 1b suggest that the way in which an earlier decision becomes relevant for some later decision in the four-stage process lies in attempted compensative behavior. That is to say, funds which were denied the agency at some earlier stage may be returned at a later stage. Such calculations are not relevant for the agency and department head decisions, since those decisions are the first and second elements of the

Table 1a. Reaction to the Present: Simple Process-incremental Behavior

Level	Equation	Hypotheses
Agency:	$w_t = \alpha_1 z_{t-1} + \varepsilon_t$	$\alpha_1 > 1.00$
Department Head:	$x_t = \beta_1 w_t + \varepsilon_t$	$0 < \beta_1 < 1.00$
Chief Municipal Administrator:	$y_t = \gamma_1 x_t + \varepsilon_t$	$0 < \gamma_1 < 1.00$
Council:	$z_t = \delta_1 y_t + \varepsilon_t$	$\delta_1 \geq 1.00$

short-term history itself. This kind of behavior does become a possibility at the third and fourth stages of the yearly process.

The first equation in Table 1b formalizes this notion for the behavior of the Chief Municipal Administrator. During the current budgetary period, the agency will have submitted its request to the department head, who will, more than likely, deny the agency a portion of its request. The Chief Municipal Administrator then makes an initial judgment on the basis of the department head's recommendation for the agency. If he feels that the magnitude of the department head's cut of the agency request was excessive, he may alter his own initial judgment by returning a portion of the cut to the agency budget. Since the quantity $(X-W)_t$ is expected to be negative, we anticipate a negative coefficient (γ_3); the resulting multiplication will yield a positive increment to the initial judgment. In addition, we do not expect the entire cut to be returned; thus $\gamma_3 > -1.00$ is anticipated.

As an agency's budget moves through each of the stages in the process for a given year, an increasing number of cuts for which compensation may be made is left in the wake. While only one cut had been made at the time of the decision taken by the Chief Municipal Administrator, the Council decisional setting provides opportunities for compensation of funds denied at two levels. Consider the equations in Table 1b which attempt to model the compensative behavior of the Council. The first equation suggests that the initial judgment made by the Council is based upon the recommendation of the Chief Municipal Administrator. The Council alters that initial judgment, however, by returning to the agency a fixed mean percentage of the difference between the agency's request and the recommendation by the Chief

Table 1b. Reaction to the Present: Process-incremental Behavior Plus Compensation for Current Year's Cuts Made Earlier in the Process

Level	Equation	Hypotheses
Agency:	—	—
Department Head:	—	—
Chief Municipal Administrator:	$y_t = \gamma_2 x_t + \gamma_3 (x-w)_t + \varepsilon_t$	$0 < \gamma_2 \leq 1.00, -1.00 < \gamma_3 < 0$
Council:	$z_t = \delta_2 y_t + \delta_3 (y-w)_t + \varepsilon_t$	$\delta_2 \geq 1.00, -1.00 < \delta_3 < 0$
	$z_t = \delta_4 y_t + \delta_5 (y-x)_t + \varepsilon_t$	$\delta_4 \geq 1.00, -1.00 < \delta_5 < 0$
	$z_1 = \delta_6 y_t + \delta_7 (y_t - z_{t-1}) + \varepsilon_t$	$\delta_6 \geq 1.00, \delta_7 < 0$

Municipal Administrator. The suggestion here is that the Council views the extent of agency cuts during the budgetary period as excessive, and attempts in part to compensate for those cuts. The second equation narrows the quantity for which the Council is willing to make compensation by focusing upon the difference between the recommendation by the Chief Municipal Administrator and that of the department head. The suggestion is that the Council is willing to make some compensation for cuts made by the Chief Municipal Administrator but that it is not willing to tamper with decisions taken by the department head.

It is useful here to note two kinds of conditions which may give rise to the choice of this decision rule. First, it is well known that the task of the Chief Municipal Administrator is to produce a unified budget within the bounds of specified fiscal constraints. If requests exceed available revenues, items from several departmental budgets are likely to be deleted. The department head, however, need not be bound by such constraints in an immediate sense. On the contrary, in preparing his recommendations, he may justify his own additions and deletions by reference to his own expertise in his sector. If the Council respects such expertise, it may hesitate to alter those decisions, but it may be more willing to compensate the agency for cuts introduced by the Chief Municipal Administrator, whose justification for such deletions may be less policy oriented.

A second condition which may lead to the choice of this decision rule involves the institutional setting itself. We have referred earlier to the practice of establishing political committees which represent the interests of each sector in the budgetary proceedings. On occasion, when an agency within the sector has been dealt a particularly hard blow by the Chief Municipal Administrator, the political committee itself may appeal to the Council in an effort to get a portion of the funds restored. When such efforts are successful, the Council will return a portion of the difference between the recommendation by the Chief Municipal Administrator and that of the department head. Thus, for the first Council equation in Table 1b, the Council returns a percentage of the entire quantity representing the total cuts introduced during the period; for the second equation, the Council compensates in part only for cuts made on the department head's decision. In either case we anticipate negative coefficients, δ_3 and δ_5, which, upon multiplication with the respective negative quantities, $(y,w)_t$ and $(y-x)_t$, will yield positive returns to the agency budget. Also, since the Council is unlikely to make complete compensation for earlier cuts, $\delta_3 > -1.00$ and $\delta_5 > -1.00$ are expected. The final Council decision equation hypothesizes that the Council exercises its own judgment with respect to proposed agency growth. If the government-proposed budget contains an excessive increase over last year's appropriation, we anticipate a cut by the Council. A proposed decrease ($y_t < z_{t-1}$), on the other hand, leads the

Council to return a portion of the funds. In either case, such decrements or increments are suggestive of Council efforts to impose a constant growth rate for the agency – consistent with a negative estimate for the parameter δ_7.

Thus far we have considered only the short-term history of events. Budgetary decision-makers, however, may probe farther into the history of their own units in search of solutions. In such cases, a series of events which took place during the budgetary proceedings of the previous year may have profound effects on decisions in the current year. Indeed, while the Chief Municipal Administrator may react primarily on the basis of the department head's recommendation for the agency in the current year, he may alter the initial judgment by taking into account the special events and circumstances existing in the previous year. The kinds of behavior which we wish to model in this third set of equations may be termed compensative and learning behavior.

Table 1c. Reactions to the Present and to the Past: Process-incremental Behavior plus Moderating the Effects of Decisions Taken in Earlier Years

Level	Equation	Hypotheses
Agency:	$w_t = \alpha_2 z_{t-1} + \alpha_3 (z-w)_{t-1} + \varepsilon_t$	$\alpha_2 > 1.00,\ \alpha_3 < 0$
		$0 < \alpha_3 < 1.00$
	$w_t = \alpha_4 z_{t-1} + \alpha_5 \Lambda_{t-1} + \varepsilon_t$	$\alpha_4 > 1.00,\ \alpha_5 < 0$
	where $\Lambda_{t-1} = w_{t-1} - \alpha z_{t-2}$	$0 < \alpha_5 < 1.00$
Department Head:	$x_t = \beta_2 w_t + \beta_3 (z-w)_{t-1} + \varepsilon_t$	$0 < \beta_2 < 1.00,\ \beta_3 < 0$
		$0 < \beta_3 < 1.00$
	$x_t = \beta_4 w_t + \beta_5 (x-w)_{t-1} + \varepsilon_t$	$0 < \beta_4 < 1.00,\ \beta_5 < 0$
		$0\qquad\qquad 0 < \beta_5 < 1.00$
	$x_t = \beta_6 w_t + \beta_7 \Lambda_{t-1} + \varepsilon_t$	$0 < \beta_6 < 1.00,\ \beta_7 < 0$
	where $\Lambda_{t-1} = x_{t-1} - \beta w_{t-1}$	$0 < \beta_7 < 1.00$
Chf Municipal Administrator:	$y_t = \gamma_4 x_t + \gamma_5 (z-w)_{t-1} + \varepsilon_t$	$0 < \gamma_4 < 1.00,\ \gamma_5 < 0$
		$0 < \gamma_5 < 1.00$
	$y_t = \gamma_6 x_t + \gamma_7 (y-w)_{t-1} + \varepsilon_t$	$0 < \gamma_6 < 1.00,\ \gamma_7 < 0$
		$0 < \gamma_7 < 1.00$
	$y_t = \gamma_8 x_t + \gamma_9 \Lambda_{t-1} + \varepsilon_t$	$0 < \gamma_8 < 1.00,\ \gamma_9 < 0$
	where $\Lambda_{t-1} = y_{t-1} - \gamma x_{t-1}$	$0 < \gamma_9 < 1.00$
Council:	$z_t = \delta_8 y_t + \delta_9 \Lambda_{t-1} + \varepsilon_t$	$\delta_8 \geq 1.00,\ \delta_9 < 0$
	where $\Lambda_{t-1} = z_{t-1} - \delta y_{t-1}$	— $\quad 0 < \delta_9 < 1.00$

We have entertained the possibility that such behavior may be observed in at least three different kinds of decision processes. First, the decision-maker may react initially to the request from the next lower level but may alter that judgment according to whatever actually happened to the agency's request in the previous year. The first equation at each of the first three levels in Table 1c models this kind of behavior. Each decision level reacts initially in a manner consistent with the notion of process-incremental behavior but alters that judgment somewhat in an effort to compensate for excessive cuts received by the agency in the previous year. With respect to the second term, $(z-w)_{t-1}$, we anticipate that the coefficients (α_3, β_3, γ_5) will not exceed unity. If any one of these coefficients is negative, we have a clear case of compensative behavior in which a positive increment is added to this year's decision in order to compensate for excessive cuts in the preceding year. If the coefficient is positive but less than unity, the attempt is to cut the agency again in the current year but by a smaller amount, given its excessive cut in the previous year. The implication is that the decision-maker is learning from, rather than compensating for, last year's experience. In particular, we may obtain such an estimate when the agency, aware of its declining importance, learns from experience in the previous year that substantial cuts will be made but attempts to minimize the effect of such cuts. For each decision rule, when two different hypotheses are indicated with regard to sign and magnitude of parameters, the first hypothesis is consistent with the notion of compensative behavior and the second with that of learning behavior.

Rather than attempting to compensate for whatever actually happened to the agency request in the previous year, the decision-maker may regard his own behavior with respect to the agency as the focus of compensation. In a sense, he may wish to 'set his own house in order', regardless of the behavior of decision-makers at other levels. This behavior is particularly relevant for the department head and the Chief Municipal Administrator, each of whom may have denied the agency a substantial portion of its request in the previous year. The second equations listed under the department head and the Chief Municipal Administrator suggest this kind of behavior. Each reacts initially to requests from the next lower level but attempts to compensate for his own excessive cuts in the previous year whenever appropriate. As for the prior set of equations, a negative coefficient associated with either the quantity $(x-w)_{t-1}$ for the department head or the quantity $(y-w)_{t-1}$ for the Chief Municipal Administrator indicates a positive increment to the current year's decision. Positive coefficients less than unity suggest that cuts continue to be introduced, but that an effort is made to lessen the magnitude of those cuts, given excessive cuts in the previous year.

The final equations for each decision-maker in Table 1c are designed to model a third type of essentially compensatory or learning behavior. They depart from the earlier equations in this section in one important respect. In the earlier two types of equations, we postulated that the decision-maker compensates for the cut itself – either his own or the total. In this final set of equations, however, we postulate that the compensation is made only for the quantity representing a departure from the usual relationship in the previous year. We assume that the usual relationship between the two proximate decision-making levels is represented by process-incremental behavior. Extraneous circumstances, represented by the residual terms, may cause a departure from that usual relationship in a given year – a departure which may be compensated for in the following year.

The previous equations represent successively greater probing efforts into the relevant history of the decision in question, with regard to both the short-term history during the current budgetary proceedings and the long-term history of relevant events in the earlier year's proceedings. Decision-makers, however, attempt not only to cope with the past but also to anticipate future consequences of their actions. In the absence of more precise information, past experience often serves as the most reliable guide for shaping expectations about future behavior. This is particularly true for the agency head, whose requests must bear the scrutiny of three different reviewers. The task is somewhat simpler for the department head who must form judgments on anticipated behavior with regard to the Chief Municipal Administrator and the Council. The task of anticipating future behavior is simplest for the Chief Municipal Administrator, who need only guess the behavior of one reviewer – the Council. Of course, this behavioral pattern is not relevant for the Council, since Council members have the final say.

We should take some care in distinguishing this fourth set of decision rules, in which past experience serves as a guide to future behavior, from the earlier set, in which past experience is a behavior to be compensated for in the present. This fourth set of equations models more genuinely gaming situations. In the first agency decision rule in Table 1d, for example, the agency requests a fixed mean percentage of its appropriation from the previous year, but that initial judgment is altered, since the agency expects a sizeable cut from the department head. Such a cue arises from the fact that the department head did, indeed, cut the agency request in the preceding year. We may raise the question, however, as to why the quantity $(z-w)_{t-1}$ in the first agency equation of Table 1c is used as a cue to compensative behavior for the past, while the quantity $(x-w)_{t-1}$ is interpreted as a cue for anticipatory behavior for the future. The answer depends, in part, on some hindsight from which we have benefited through an initial examination of these data. It is almost always true that the Council appropriations for these agencies exceed the amount requested by the Chief Municipal Administrator in the government's budget. If we examine successive differences in each level for a given agency in year t, the prevailing pattern with respect to agency requests is the following: substantial cuts by the department head, moderate cuts of the departmental recommendation by the Chief Municipal Administrator, and small additions to the government-proposed budget by the Council.

Given this pattern, use of the quantity $(z-w)_{t-1}$ as a guide to future behavior is not recommended for the simple reason that its interpretation is confused by the inclusion of both additions and deletions to the agency request. An agency may wish to compensate for whatever actually happened to its request in the previous year regardless of which level introduced subsequent additions or deletions. In attempting to anticipate future consequences, however, the level and the magnitude at each level become relevant. The use of the quantity $(z-w)_{t-1}$ is not appropriate; rather it is necessary to distinguish between the levels at which deletions may be expected and those at which additions may be expected.

Table 1d. Reactions to the Present and to the Future: Process-incremental Behavior plus Anticipating Future Behavior

Level	Equation	Hypotheses
Agency:	$w_t = \alpha_6 z_{t-1} + \alpha_7 (x-w)_{t-1} + \varepsilon_t$	$\alpha_6 > 1.00, \alpha_7 < 0$ $0 < \alpha_7 < 1.00$
	$w_t = \alpha_8 z_{t-1} + (\alpha_9 + \alpha_{10}\Omega_{t-1})(y-w)_{t-1} + \varepsilon_t$ where $\Omega_{t-1} = +1$ if $(z-y)_{t-1} > 0$, $\Omega_{t-1} = 0$ if $(z-y)_{t-1} = 0$, $\Omega_{t-1} = -1$ if $(z-y)_{t-1} < 0$.	$\alpha_8 > 1.00, \alpha_9 < 0, \alpha_{10} > 0$ $\alpha_9 > 0, \alpha_{10} < 0$
Department Head:	$X_t = \beta_8 w_t + \beta_9 (y-x)_{t-1} + \varepsilon_t$	$0 < \beta_8 < 1.00, \beta_9 < 0$ $0 < \beta_9 < 1.00$
	$x_t = \beta_{10} w_t + (\beta_{11} + \beta_{12}\Omega_{t-1})(y-x)_{t-1} + \varepsilon_t$ with Ω_{t-1} as defined above.	$0 < \beta_{10} < 1.00, \beta_{11} < 0, \beta_{12} > 0$ $\beta_{11} > 0, \beta_{12} < 0$
Chf Municipal Administrator:	$y_t = \gamma_{10} x_t + \gamma_{11}(z-y)_{t-1} + \varepsilon_t$	$0 < \gamma_{10} < 1.00, \gamma_{11} < 0$ $0 < \gamma_{11} < 1.00$
Council:		

We have formulated the equations in Table 1d from what we know about the prevailing pattern of cuts and increases at each of the levels. The first agency equation is drawn from the perspective that, in almost every case, the most substantial cuts occur during the departmental review. Thus, agency thinking may be dominated by the problem of guessing future behavior at that level. Comparable behavior is suggested for the department head, who must anticipate sizeable cuts only by the Chief Municipal Administrator. The lone equation for the Chief Municipal Administrator in Table 1d indicates that there is but one level – the Council – at which future behavior must be anticipated. For each of these equations at the three levels, the sign of the coefficients for the second term is indicative of the type of behavioral pattern. For the agency and departmental equations, negative coefficients (α_7 and β_9) yield positive increments to initial decisions – reflecting efforts to compensate in advance for cuts expected in the future. For the Chief Municipal Administrator equation, a negative value for the coefficient, γ_{11}, would indicate a net decrement to the initial decision – reflecting an effort to compensate in advance for funds likely to be returned to the agency by the Council. Nonetheless, negative values for the coefficients, α_7, β_9 and γ_{11}, suggest anticipatory behavior. Positive coefficients less than unity indicate that the decisional unit has learned that alterations will be made, but it attempts to smooth out the effects of such anticipated changes.

The second agency and departmental equations in Table 1d are designed to model more complex gaming behavior. As we have suggested earlier, the task of anticipating future behavior during a given budgetary period is most difficult for the agency and for the department head, who must guess future budgetary decisions at three and two levels respectively. The peculiar perspective which is brought to that decisional setting by one of those levels – the Council – focuses upon the return of funds previously deleted rather than upon continued cuts. For the second agency equation in Table 1d, we postulate that the agency chief requests a fixed mean percentage of his appropriations in the previous year; however, he will attempt to compensate for the expected total cut after review by the department head and by the Chief Municipal Administrator. The magnitude of that compensation is dependent upon whether the Council can be expected to return a portion of those deleted funds. Thus, we may conceive of the coefficient to be attached to the quantity $(y-w)_{t-1}$, as possessing any one of three different values which are themselves monotonically related. First, the variable Ω_{t-1} is simply a dummy variable for which a positive value indicates that the Council returned funds to the agency over the recommendation of the Chief Municipal Administrator. If the agency expects such restorative behavior by the Council, the required compensation will be less for expected cuts. Alternatively, if the agency anticipates further cuts by the Council, the required compensation will be even greater. Finally, if the agency expects the Council to accept the recommendation of the Chief Municipal Administrator ($\Omega_{t-1} = 0$), then it need only compensate for anticipated cuts up through the review by the Chief Municipal Administrator. By representing expected Council behavior as a dummy variable, we achieve a more natural behavioral interpretation of parameter estimates for the decision rule. For example, the coefficient ($\alpha_9 + \alpha_{10}\Omega_{t-1}$) may possess three alternative values which vary in a manner consistent with the notion that compensative behavior is less important when the Council restores depleted funds than when it continues to cut them. Note that the type of learning behavior suggested above may be relevant here if the pattern of the coefficient signs is the reverse. Note also that the comparable complex gaming behavior is suggested for the department head.[5]

Model Selection Criteria and Measurement

The different decision rules we have specified in the previous section are based on the assumption that the relationships between the dependent and independent variables at all levels in the budgetary process can be described by simple linear equations. The parameters of the equations have been estimated by ordinary least-squares regression methods. The tests used to evaluate the models are based on the assumption that the dependent variable in each equation is a stochastic variable with a normal distribution. Strictly speaking our sample of observations is not a random sample. With such a sample, one might suggest discarding tests of significance and making use of prior information about budgeting in order to decide what is or is not a significant relationship. Unfortunately, the subtleties of the strategies we wish to model as well as the sheer number of postulated equations precluded such an approach. Thus, we rely on tests of significance for lack of a better alternative – a procedure for which we find ample justification suggested by its frequency in the econometric literature.[6]

Tables 1a-d in the previous section contain several possible decision equations for each level in the budgetary process. The confrontation of these theoretical equations with a series of observations over time posed some rather complex questions with regard to the choice of one best-fitting equation for each agency at each level. First we examined the set of complex equations, selecting from those equations the subset for which the coefficients for complex behavior were significant at the five percent level. Those complex equations with nonsignificant coefficients were eliminated from further consideration. The simple equation was chosen when none of the coefficients for complex behavior met this level of significance for the t test. These tests were based upon estimated parameters for which the regression plane is constrained to pass through the origin. For the remaining set of equations, we examined the behavior of the constant term itself. A convincing application of these models depends upon such a test, since the natural percentage interpretation of the parameter estimates follows only from a zero (within sampling error) value for the constant term. An estimate of the constant term which is significantly different from zero suggests that something is awry with the model in question. Those equations were deleted from further consideration.

One of the main difficulties in analyses involving time series data is the problem of serial correlation in the error terms for a given equation. Therefore, as a third criterion the Durbin-Watson test (at the 5 percent significance level) for serial correlation in the estimated residual values was used when appropriate.[7] Thus we further eliminated from the set under consideration those equations for which we found significant serial correlation. For the remaining equations, a fourth and final criterion was applied – the maximum sample correlation coefficient between predicted and actual values of the dependent variable.[8]

Consonant with the symbolic representation in Tables 1a-d, we define the following empirical quantities (each expressed in thousands of Norwegian kroner):

w_t = the appropriation requested by the agency in year t
x_t = the appropriation recommended for the agency by the department head in year t
y_t = the appropriation proposed for the agency in the government budget by the Chief Municipal Administrator in year t
z_t = the appropriation passed for the agency by the Council in year t

Time-series data on each of these four items were collected for each agency over the nineteen-year period from 1953 through 1971.[9] Although data are available prior to 1953, we have excluded that time period because of the confounding effects of post-war economic restrictions which existed in some form until 1952.

Empirical Results

We have conceptualized a series of budgetary events as a process. It is useful, therefore, to illustrate how each decisional element may be fitted together as a means of describing the decision history of a given unit, before moving on to the more general question of applicability across these forty-seven agencies. A brief consideration of one such set is illustrative of how such an analysis may proceed. Consider the equations describing the decision history of the Education Department's Administrative Body:[10]

Agency: $w_t = 1.2763(z)_{t-1} + e_t$
Department: $x_t = .9136(w)_t - .4121(y-x)_{t-1} + e_t$
Chief Municipal Administrator: $y_t = .9482(x)_t + e_t$
Council: $z_t = .9932(y_t) - .2883(y-x)_t + e_t$

First it is clear that the agency is rather acquisitive in formulating its yearly requests; on the average, it has sought a yearly increase of about 28 percent. The initial judgment by the department head is that the agency actually should receive, on the average, about 91 percent of its request. Generally, however, the department head recommends a bit more for the agency than is indicated by this initial judgment in an effort to anticipate future behavior on the part of the Chief Municipal Administrator. Since the department head expects a substantial cut (with the behavior of the Chief Municipal Administrator in the previous year serving as a cue), he augments his initial judgment. Note that the multiplication of the negative coefficient ($ß_9 = -.4121$) by the negative quantity $(y-x)_{t-1}$ yields such a positive increment. Such a strategy by the department head is wisely chosen in light of the actual behavior of the Chief Municipal Administrator, who grants, on the average, about 95 per cent of the recommendation – a rather low percentage in comparison to the percentages granted to remaining agencies. Finally, the Council leaves the government-proposed budget almost intact in this case – granting about 100 per cent of the recommendation by the Chief Municipal Administrator. The Council, however, compensates the agency for the excessive cuts – returning on the average about a quarter of the funds deleted by the Chief Municipal Administrator. Note that the Council apparently accepts the cuts made by the department head, reflecting perhaps an acceptance of the department head's expertise in his own policy sector. Yet, the Council is quite willing to make substantial allowance for cuts imposed by the Chief Municipal Administrator, who probably cannot marshal so credible a case for reducing the agency budget.

(1) Within the bounds of a small random error, budgetary data for these forty-seven agencies of the Oslo municipal government are consistent with the hypothesis that agency chiefs, department heads, the

Chief Municipal Administrator, and the Council arrive at budgetary decisions through the utilization of one of a set of linear decision rules. The parameters of each of the decision equations in Tables 1a-d were estimated for each agency, and the criteria indicated in the previous section as well as the hypotheses concerning the signs and magnitudes of the coefficients were utilized to arrive at a best-fitting decision rule for each agency at each level in the process. The array of squared multiple correlation coefficients in Table 2 supports the hypothesis that budgetary decisions at each of the four levels for these forty-seven agencies of the Oslo municipal government are linear and stable over

Table 2. Distribution of Squared Multiple Correlation Coefficients for Best-fitting Decision Equations by Level in the Budgetary Process

Level	\multicolumn{8}{c}{Squared Multiple Correlation Coefficient}
	1.000 -	.990 -	.980 -	.970 -	.960 -	.950 -	.940 -	.800 - less than .800
Agency	3	6	5	3	5	4	11	10
Department Head	40	3	1	0	0	0	2	1
Chief Municipal Administrator	36	3	2	2	1	0	2	1
Council	41	4	0	0	1	0	1	0

time. An exceedingly large proportion of the total variance is explained in each case. An outstanding property of Table 2, however, is the distinctive aspect of behavior at the agency level in comparison to the remaining three levels. The multiple correlations for the agency equations are typically lower than those for the remaining three levels. A variety of factors may explain the distinctiveness of agency behavior in this regard – the influence of external demands arising from each agency's environment, cues from higher level reviewing agents which weaken the link between last year's appropriation and this year's request, or any of several political considerations not specified in these models.

(2) The internal bureaucratic aspects of budgetary behavior become more complex as one moves up the levels of the administrative hierarchy. The finding is not an obvious one, and our prior knowledge of budgetary processes suggested two conflicting patterns. In this analysis the lowest unit in the administrative hierarchy is the agency itself. This means that the agency's task is most difficult from the standpoint of arriving at a request figure which can bear up under the scrutiny of three successive reviewers. Departmental behavior need be

somewhat less complex and the behavior of the Chief Municipal Administrator is likely to be simplest from this standpoint. An alternative perspective is suggested by focusing upon the task itself rather than upon the strategy. An agency chief need only formulate a budget request for his own unit, while the department head must coordinate requests from several agencies. Finally, the task for the Chief Municipal Administrator becomes very complex as he works over all departmental requests for individual agencies in each department in an effort to produce the final government-proposed budget. We find support in these data for the second perspective.

The percentage calculations in Table 3 are based upon the choice of one best-fitting decision rule for each agency and are classified according to the time-dimension distinctions suggested in Tables 1a-d. Entries in the first column of the table indicate the percentage of the total decisions (47) at the given level which can be best described as simple process-incremental behavior. Remaining entries partition complex behavior with regard to the time dimension which provides the reference point for the complex decision in question. If the three administrative levels are distinguished from the legislative level, it is clear from the table that budgetary behavior becomes more complex as the administrative level increases.

These estimates provide us with an opportunity to examine, in gross terms, the policy consequences of strategic behavior. By policy consequences from a budgetary standpoint, we are not referring to specific programs, but rather to the growth in expenditures for a given agency's set of activities. Thus, expenditures for the activities of some agencies may grow at a faster rate than others, by virtue of the type of strategy chosen and in contrast to steering attempts by the government. At least two properties of the above estimated linear equations are amenable to this kind of formulation – the complexity and the acquisitiveness of agency-reviewer strategies. By complexity, we mean the number of elements in the estimated decision structure; and we form a dichotomous variable, with observations by agency, which indicates whether the strategy has been one of simple process incrementalism or of a more complex form. One of the consequences of more conscious gaming behavior on the part of the agency ought to be payoffs in the form of higher growth rates for the agency's activities. We define this average growth rate over the nineteen-year period by the following:

$$Z_{1i} \cdot (1 \cdot p_i)^{18} = Z_{19}$$

where p_i is the mean growth rate for agency i.

(3) The complexity of the agency-reviewer strategies is not related to

Table 3. Type of Best-fitting Equation by Level in the Budgetary Process

	Simple	Complex			
Level	process incrementalism	process incrementalism plus short-term past	process incrementalism plus long-term past	process incrementalism plus anticipating future behavior	total (N)
Agency:	72%	+	17%	11%	100% (47)
Department Head:	64	+	23	13	100 (47)
Chief Municipal Administrator:	53	13	26	9	101 (47)
Council:	57	40	2	+	99 (47)

+ inapplicable

the agency's average growth rate over time. Table 4 shows the simple relationships between the complexity of strategies at each level in the budgetary process and agency growth, as well as the relationships between strategy complexity at each level. While these estimates may be somewhat attenuated because of the dichotomous nature of the complexity variables, the results are reasonably clear on one point: A more complex gaming strategy does not increase the probability for long-term budget success; a simple incremental strategy is equally beneficial. Nor are complex strategies at subsequent levels, the exception being the strategic links between the Chief Municipal Administrator and the Council. It is significant that several of these complex equations for the Chief Municipal Administrator suggest anticipating future additions, by the Council, to his recommendation; and, in all of these save one, the Council strategy, indeed, indicated the restoration of funds, with the magnitude of deletions by the Chief Municipal Administrator serving as a guide.

(4) The more acquisitive the agency strategy, the higher the actual growth rate. Intermediate reviewing levels are partially successful

Table 4. Relationships Between Strategy Complexity and Long-term Growth by Level in the Budgetary Process*

	Complexity:			
	Agency	Department Head	Chief Municipal Adm.	City Council
Average Growth Rate	-.012	-.115	-.230	-.128
Complexity: Agency		.030	.087	-.051
Complexity: Department Head			.181	.248*
Complexity: Chief Municipal Adm.				.400*
Complexity: City Council				

* Pearson product-moment correlation coefficients; N = 47.
* Significant at .05 level.

in identifying particularly acquisitive agencies and reducing their intended growth rates. Earlier work on budgetary processes in the United States has stressed the point that a set of mutual expectations develops among participants over time. Some agencies expect that substantial cuts will be made in their requests and pad those requests accordingly. Others, with a rather noble image among reviewing agents, may pad only slightly with the expectation of few or no cuts. Reviewing agents presumably develop comparable views of those agencies – slashing severely those suspected of excessive attempts at expansion, and altering others only slightly. If a budgetary system is functioning in the manner suggested by this theoretical perspective, there ought to be no relationship between the acquisitiveness of the agency's strategy and its actual growth rate – since those agencies which are relatively acquisitive or expansive from year to year will be those which come to receive the severest cuts by reviewing agents. Such a system will reach an equilibrium point in which agencies pursuing highly acquisitive strategies will not, on the average, experience higher actual growth rates than do agencies pursuing less acquisitive strategies.

We have an opportunity to test such a proposition for these forty-seven agencies in the Oslo municipal government. The required quantities are immediately available from the parameter estimates for the simple equations in Table 1a. These parameter estimates for each agency serve as observations which summarize several properties of agency-reviewer relationships over the nineteen-year period:

α_{1i} = average percent increase in expenditures requested by agency i over the nineteen-year period or, agency acquisitiveness.
β_{1i} = average percent of agency i's request recommended by the department head over the nineteen-year period.
γ_{1i} = average percent of department head's recommendation for agency i recommended by the Chief Municipal Administrator over the nineteen-year period.
δ_{1i} = average percent of Chief Municipal Administrator's recommendation for agency i appropriated by the council over the nineteen-year period.

Our expectations may be formalized:

$r\alpha\beta < 0$ and/or $r\alpha\gamma < 0$
$r_p\alpha \cong 0$
$r_p\alpha\cdot\beta > 0$
$r_p\alpha\cdot\beta\ \gamma > r_p\alpha\cdot\beta > 0$

Simple relationships between mean growth rate, agency acquisitiveness, and subsequent action by appropriate reviewing agents are presented in Table 5a. It is clear from those entries that the expansive character of the agency strategy is an important determinant of agency growth. The more acquisitive the agency, the higher its actual growth rate over the nineteen-year period. Support at each of the three levels of budgetary review is only slightly related to actual agency growth –

perhaps in contrast to Sharkansky's findings for the American states for which support by the state governor appears crucial.[11] It is significant to note, however, that highly acquisitive agencies do receive their severest treatment from the Chief Municipal Administrator ($r\alpha\ \gamma$ = -0.371), who, because of the constitutional requirements of producing a balanced budget, appears to be led rather naturally to the most expansive agencies.

Table 5a. Relationships Between Agency Acquisitiveness, Average Growth Rate, and Actions by Intermediate Budgetary Reviewers*

		α_1	β_1	γ_1	δ_1
Average Growth Rate:	p	.411*	.225	.249*	-.237
Agency Acquisitiveness:	α_1		-.259	-.371	.164
Department Head:	β_1			.388*	-.447*
Chief Municipal Adm.:	γ_1				-.472*
City Council:	δ_1				

* Pearson product-moment correlation coefficients; N = 47.
* Significant at .05 level.

The pattern of coefficients relating Council action to the remaining variables is an interesting one, for it is suggestive of the subtleties of political influence on a process which often appears to be markedly deterministic. Those agencies which over the nineteen-year period have received the most unfavorable treatment by the department head and the Chief Municipal Administrator have been the principal beneficiaries of Council action at the final stage of review ($r\delta\beta$ = -0.447 and $r\gamma\beta$ = -0.472)Yet the relationship between agency acquisitiveness and Council restorative action is on expansive agencies which have been treated severely by their intermediate budgetary reviewers – a role not unlike that often attributed to the U.S. Senate in budgetary considerations.[12]

The entries in Table 5b are more directly applicable to the hypothesis that actions by intermediate reviewing agents serve to reduce the relationship between the acquisitiveness of the agency strategy and actual growth rates. The problem lends itself rather naturally to formulation in the interpretative language of higher-order partial correlation coefficients. We first examine the simple correlation between agency acquisitiveness and long-term growth. The hypothesis is that the action of intermediate reviewing levels serves to weaken that relationship; in other words, the relationship between agency acquisitiveness and long-term growth would be much stronger were it not for the patterned practice of the department head and the Chief Municipal Administrator to distribute their cuts disproportionately to the most acquisitive agen-

Table 5b. Relationship Between Agency Acquisitiveness and Average Growth Rate, Controlling for Actions by Intermediate Budgetary Reviewers.

		Controlling for Actions by:	
Agency Acquisitiveness and Average Growth	Department Head	Department Head and Chief Municipal Adm.	Department Head, Chief Municipal Adm., and City Council
.411	.499	.590	.588

cies. The expectation is that the magnitude of that correlation coefficient increases as controls are introduced successively for action by higher level participants in the process. As the entries in Table 5b indicate, a control introduced for action by the department head effectively increases the magnitude from +0.411 to +0.499. Furthermore, when action by both the department head and the Chief Municipal Administrator are removed, the value of the partial correlation reaches a magnitude of +0.590. Note that further control for Council action shows negligible effects.

These findings suggest two important conclusions concerning the acquisitive nature of an agency's strategy and its actual growth rate. First, we do find support for the view that administrative reviewing agents select the most expansive agencies as recipients of the severest cuts. As the pattern of partial correlations suggests, the relationship between acquisitiveness and growth would be much stronger were it not for actions taken during the process by the department head and the Chief Municipal Administrator. As this pattern, however, is juxtaposed alongside the value of the simple correlation itself, a second conclusion is indicated. Although intermediate reviewing levels are partially successful in blunting the effect of acquisitiveness on actual growth, they are not entirely successful; a moderately strong correlation obtains between agency acquisitiveness and actual growth, regardless of action taken by intermediate reviewers in the budgetary process. Simply put, an expansive strategy will pay off for the agency in the long run – even though intermediate percentage cuts will be more severe.

Any number of factors, unmeasured at this point, could account for the observed pattern. The problem may be essentially an informational one. If an agency is in the habit of padding its yearly request, the department head and the Chief Municipal Administrator are likely to be aware of that practice. Yet, the determination of just what portion of the agency request represents padding is difficult. There is likely to be a good deal of slippage here. Large cuts may be introduced at these subsequent levels but, given informational inadequacies, those cuts may not compensate sufficiently for excessive agency padding. Alternatively, the observed pattern may suggest the presence of more conscious steering on the part of the government itself than our decision models take into account. Agencies may be acquisitive or expansive as a direct result of cues received from higher level government decision makers – with the natural result that such stimulated acquisitiveness is accepted by the government.

Conclusions, Reservations, and Prospects for Future Research

While this study owes its intellectual genesis to a set of theoretical materials developed for the American setting, both design and conclusion suggest an important point of departure. We began with a reservation about restricting the formulations to relationships between government and legislature as well as a genuine interest in action at lower levels in the process. We strongly suspected that most of the action occurred earlier in that process, with alterations of relatively small magnitude at the point of legislative review. Our analysis of time-series budgetary data for the Oslo municipal government at four different levels in the process confirms that perspective: substantial alterations in agency requests by the department head are followed by additional, moderate alterations by the Chief Municipal Administrator, whose final decision is only marginally changed by the Municipal Council. We suspect that studies of budgeting in other systems, particularly the parliamentary systems of Western Europe, will need to probe beyond the government-legislature nexus, perhaps in contrast to the requirements for research in American budgetary processes.

We also find support in these data for the proposition that reciprocal strategic decision models is as applicable in the Norwegian as in the American setting. Very little of the variance at each of the four levels in the budgetary process remains unexplained. We have observed several decisional properties which highlight the necessity of examining in detail strategic behavior at each level. Strategic conditions become more complex at higher levels of the administrative hierarchy, although the complexity of the strategy itself is not related to long-term growth. We find the largest concentration of simple incremental strategies at the agency level.

We find also support in these data for the proposition that reciprocal expectations develop among participants over the long run such that intermediate reviewers cut most severely the requests of those agencies which attempt to be the most expansive. From this viewpoint it is useful to recall a quotation from Wildavsky's earlier work.[13]

> ... if they ask for amounts much larger than the appropriating bodies believe reasonable, the agencies' credibility will suffer a drastic decline. In such circumstances, the reviewing organs are likely to cut deeply, with the result that the agency gets much less than it might have with a more moderate request. So the first guide for decision is: do not come in too high.

We cannot comment on the last statement, which implies that decision-makers actually follow such a guide for decision; however, our results concerning the relationship between agency acquisitiveness and long-term growth rather clearly indicate that such a guide for decision is needlessly restrictive. Certainly in terms of action by reviewing agents, percentage cuts will be more severe for the acquisitive than for the nonacquisitive agency. The magnitude of that cut, however, is not sufficient to produce comparable growth rates for acquisitive and nonacquisitive agencies; the acquisitive budgeter holds the advantage.

Such observed patterns may be suggestive of system properties arising from the wider political order. The institutionalization of the Scandinavian welfare state has created a receptivity to the appropriateness of government spending in a variety of areas. The phenomenon of an ever-expanding government budget is much more common in Scandinavia than in most municipalities in the United States, where fiscal as well as ideological factors have operated to hold the line on government spending. Indeed, one important property of systems more receptive to high levels of government spending may be a certain hesitancy on the part of reviewers to make substantial deletions in requests by their administrative units. We suspect, also, that another important factor distinguishes budgetary processes in Oslo from those in many American cities – the consistency and pervasiveness, if not the magnitude, of legislative restorations to depleted agency requests. Through such action, the Labor-dominated City Council may be able to provide clear signals of political priorities – encouraging some agencies to be quite expansive in their requests and discouraging in some cases severe action by administrative reviewers with the threat of legislative restoration.

This analysis strategy departs from that in earlier chapters in several respects. First, we have observed elements in a process overtime rather than cross-sectionally. Second, by incorporating actual quantities and subsequently estimating percentages with these formulations, we have extended the analysis by focusing on budget base as well as on budget change. Third, we have been able to single out those properties of behavior which show some stability over a considerable period of time. The point that we have not tried to test the same hypotheses with a different kind of data deserves re-emphasis. Rather, our perspective has been the following: some questions are best answered with cross-sectional interview/questionnaire data; other questions require observations over a more extended period of time – even at the loss of some perceptual information which can never be reconstructed for past events. Apart from the testing of specific hypotheses, however, the results of these two analyses can be brought together from one standpoint: To what extent do both support broader, more general interpretations of the politics of budgeting. In the final chapter, we try to answer that question.

The interplay between cross-sectional and time series analysis is not as limited as the above remarks might suggest. We have found it useful on occasion to utilize one set of results in testing the assumptions of the alternative mode of analysis. For example, while we believe the evidence presented above to be sufficient to justify our conclusions thus far, we have tried to avoid acceptance with an uncritical eye. In retrospect, a number of assumptions may be thought of as necessary conditions for the valid application of these models. Perhaps the most fundamental assumption lies at the interface between the theoretical propositions we have sought to test and the data brought to bear on those propositions – the assumption of cognition. The interpretative logic of these models depends upon the assumption that decision-makers actually think about budgetary problems in percentage terms. We have not, as yet, presented any evidence bearing upon that kind of cognitive assumption at the level of the individual decision-maker, nor are we aware of any systematic evidence on this point from similar studies. It is entirely possible to obtain the pattern of results above with any of several alternative styles of decision-making – thinking in terms of monetary units, simply adding new programs to the agency budget, increasing one program by a specified amount, etc.

For this purpose we are able to draw upon our set of interview-questionnaire materials in testing some of the underlying assumptions of these linear decision models. More specifically, if decision-makers engage in the kind of problem-solving implied by these models, then a necessary condition is that they have some recollection of the elements of that postulated decision structure: the requested increase last year; the percentage alternations by department head, Chief Municipal Ad-

Table 6. Cognition by Individual Agency Officials of Elements in the Postulated Decision Structure

Element: Type of Element: Response:	precise percentage figure	percentage range	monetary amount	don't know/ remember	Total	(N)
% cut by dept. head	53%	15%	1%	31%	100%	(85)
% cut by Chief Municipal Adm.	55	13	1	31	100	(85)
% change by Council	65	5	5	25	100	(81)
% increase requested	51	20	4	25	100	(84)
% request received	60	13	4	24	101	(85)
% prediction	66	18	1	15	100	(83)

ministrator, and Council; the overall percentage cut; as well as some judgment as to how the request is likely to fare in the upcoming budget considerations. Considerable care was taken in the interview setting in obtaining these responses. The respondent was introduced to this series of questions by the following: 'We'd like to ask you to recall, in as much detail as possible, the actions concerning your budgetary requests last year. We realize that some points you will recall quite clearly but that others you won't be able to remember. Please feel free simply to tell us if you don't remember certain things.' In this way we hope to distinguish between those elements of the decision structure which lie at the surface of individual cognizance and those which do not.

The entries in Table 6 indicate that in a substantial majority of the cases, the cognitive requirements of these models are indeed met. About two-thirds of our respondents appear to have a clear recollection of these various aspects of budgetary action in percentage terms for the preceding year and are able to give some prediction about what they expect to happen in the upcoming year – some responding in terms of a narrow range but most with a precise percentage figure. We cannot, however, ignore the roughly one-third to one-fourth of the cases concentrated in the don't know categories of the table; and here the interpretation is quite clear. About one-third to one-fourth of these agency officials do not meet even the minimal cognitive requirements of recall regarding the principal elements of the model decision structure.[14] This should not, however, detract from the general finding that a substantial majority do meet those requirements. If we extrapolate from the cross-sectional to the time series data, we would expect not to be in error in about two-thirds of the cases – an extrapolation which we feel easily justifies the use of these models from this standpoint.

The results of this test, taken in conjunction with the distinctly lower levels of explained variance for the agency decision equations, provide ample justification for our earlier foray into the perceptions, evaluations and behaviors of agency officials themselves. A restricted reliance on budgetary data overtime will tell us some important things about budgeting; indeed, some questions are best answered with such data. Yet, more subtle, although pervasive, effects of other kinds of factors will remain concealed. In still other cases, we would have been just plain wrong – namely, in those cases for which the assumptions of these formulations simply do not hold. In retrospect, we should not have suspected otherwise; for it is unlikely indeed that the elusive processes of financial resource allocation decisions could be captured with any single-pronged analytic/research strategy.

VIII. Budgeting Systems: The Potential for Change

In this final chapter, we want to depart briefly from the rigidities of our data by speculating about some of the broader implications of our findings. We have tried to remain sensitive throughout to the temporal and locational dependencies of the findings from this study. But, in a broader sense, most careful studies suffer from such dependencies. We want to speak now of budgeting as if our findings were valid across time and space – leaving to the reader and to other investigators the question of validity for other governmental settings.

If our findings point us in one new direction on an issue for which other studies have been, at a minimum, ambiguous, it is toward the view of budgeting as a highly volatile and dynamic process. Yet, we find this volatility to be ultimately explicable with reference to important political, economic and social forces in communities. Many of the research questions we have raised are not new; they have justly gained, in one form or another, the attention of scholars for some time. We shall try to set our findings in this broader context – not by reviewing systematically the development of this voluminous literature but by focusing on representative studies which depict its major strains. These major issues center upon the concepts of incrementalism and change, partisanship, and socio-economic context. We deal with each in turn.

There is no concept more prevalent in research on public spending than that of incrementalism. Wildavsky provides the best and the brightest statement of it:[1]

> Budgeting is incremental, not comprehensive. The beginning of wisdom about an agency budget is that it is almost never actively reviewed as a whole every year in the sense of reconsidering the value of all existing programs as compared to all possible alternatives. Instead, it is based on last year's budget with special attention given to a narrow range of increases or decreases. Thus the men who make the budget are concerned with relatively small increments to an existing base.

Yet, as so often happens with respect to major contributions, subsequent analysts overstate the commitment of the original work to a particular line of argument; straw men proliferate. As we re-read *The Politics of the Budgetary Process,* we were struck with the compatibility of its findings with our own. We find little in it which proclaims impotency, sterility, and determinism in budgeting at the expense of political volatility, conflict, and bargaining. We find, rather, a view which suggests that some elements of budgeting are quite stable and repetitive, others quite volatile and unique. Incrementalism holds that changes will be made in the margins. We have sought to explain the magnitudes of these kinds of changes. From this view, budgeting is both incremental and subject to important sources of environmental and political change.

The concept of incrementalism is often discussed as if it were taken to mean mindless, insignificant, deterministic decision-making – the polar opposite of a decisional context in which policy-makers exert meaningful, programmatic control over the direction of government spending. Such a view is, of course, neeedlessly excessive. Marginal, nondramatic change occurs in most agencies in most developed societies; but the explanation of the varying magnitudes of those margins remains an important political and policy problem.

This brings us to a second issue of considerable importance in Western democracies – the relevance of political parties, the central organizations which organize our politics, for the actual formation of government policy. We have argued that, while much in budgeting remains stable, much change in public spending is significantly related to the stances of political parties. Davis, Dempster, and Wildavsky come to similar conclusions with different research methods in a very different governmental setting – the American national government.[2] Expanding on their initial set of linear decision models, Davis *et al.* show changes in Administration party do have a significant effect on public spending in a number of instances. We are only beginning to demonstrate the significance of party for public spending in Western democracies; but, that such effects are evident in two such disparate settings on a set of activities as complex as budgeting suggests that parties in these systems do have meaningful and vital roles to play in directing public spending.

Finally, a central issue in studies of budgeting has been the relevance of broader social and economic environments for public spending. We have found evidence of significant group and clientele input in budgeting in Oslo. Yet, two other important studies of local budgeting in different settings show findings in some contrast to our own. Olsen's study of local budgeting in a small Norwegian commune indicates that few interest groups were activated during the period of budget deliberations;[3] and, Crecine's computer simulation of budgeting in three large American cities supports the view of budgeting as a process largely insulated and isolated from external pressure.[4] It is simply too early to say whether these differences have to do with varying city sizes or with national variations in partisan and interest conflict. Yet, the question of the openness of policy-making structures to important interests and cleavages in societies remains an important question and an important theme in this literature.

All of these studies of budgeting seem predicated on the assumption that in one way or another, it is necessary to understand the nature of change in government decision processes. The incrementalist discovers little and dispairs of its insignificance; the student of political parties finds parties ill-equipped to handle and unable to direct trends in government spending as they confront larger and larger bureaucracies and a maze of proliferating government programs; and, the organization theorist discovers bureaucracies so well entrenched as to become insensitive to the needs and demands of the people they ostensibly serve. The implications of these views are extraordinary for, at a higher level of generalization, they tell us of the inability of political man to control the mechanisms which he himself establishes for purposes of societal steering. We want to confront this dilemma, in the light of our own findings, from the twin standpoints of the initiation of change and the acceptance of change.

The Initiation of Change

Change in resource allocation is rarely a function of one decision, one event, one condition, or one actor. Rather, changes in the end-product are very much the result of sequences of decisions, a complex of events, a veriety of conditions, and the interactions of multiple actors. We may, nonetheless, impose some order on these interdependencies by returning to our alternative conceptualizations of change set out in Chapter II: (1) change as reflected in comparisons of existing states of nature with preferred future states, and (2) change as reflected in comparisons of alternative future states. We term the end-products of these comparisons, more popularly, the initiation of change and the direction of change.

The decisional exercise in which individuals compare their existing states of nature with their preferred states of nature is manifested in budgeting predominantly at the lower levels – in the actions, judgments, and choices of individual agency officials themselves. These officials, closest to the policy relevant conditions in society for their agency activities, are simply more likely to initiate change; and they do so in varying degrees by attempting to expand their budgets.

Such decisions represent conscious choices of individuals to alter their states of nature, and we have sought to understand some of the determinants of those choices. First, the acquisitiveness of those decisions seems strongly tied to the judgments of agency officials about the satisfactions and dissatisfactions of individuals directly affected by the programs, activities, and services of their agencies. Indeed, the willingness of these officials to make judgments of this kind and to link those judgements with the magnitudes of their budget requests provide one of the most important elements of the environment-government nexus. Judgments of human conditions outside government shape allocation choices within.

Second, strategic considerations lead directly to the initiation of change at lower levels. Budgetary manifestations of preferred changes are often more dramatic than would be expected; and at least a portion of the explanation for that lies in the parallel expectation that one must request more for budget expansions than one fully expects to receive. Such calculations typically devolve upon the cumulative experiences of successes and failures spanning a number of years of budgeting experience.

Finally, structural variations associated with the organizations and activities of individual agencies seem to bear importantly on the initiation of change. Agencies which can draw upon the technological capabilities of their own planning units appear to generate more expansive budgets. In addition, smaller agencies – perhaps for strategic reasons – and agencies whose activities are most free from national governmental restrictions seem somewhat more acquisitive in their efforts to expand their expenditure bases.

We may view the results of these initiations of change by lower level officials as a setting of the context in which higher level administrative and political leaders steer the direction of community resource allocations. The opportunities for change are determined by the options for change set out by individual agency officials closest to the policy problems of their units; but the acceptance, rejection, or direction of change is ultimately set by an administrative and political leadership who compare their preferred states of nature with those preferred by the initiators of change.

The Direction of Change

The relationship between acceptance and rejection of initiations for change and the important political, economic, and social forces in societies reflects the operation of one of the most important mechanisms by which political man steers the institutions which he establishes. It is at this juncture that the political vitality of public budgeting becomes ultimately dependent upon the political vitality of the society in which public institutions exist. Administrative units do not simply receive what they ask for; but, rather, their fates are very much dependent upon the preferences, activities, and support of political parties and interests in those societies.

Competition among political parties, each holding varying views of appropriate activities for government in society, provides one of the most important elements in democratic theory in the Western tradition. The process of budgeting in which the allocation of public financial resources takes place under the eyes of democratically elected representatives constitutes one of the most important derivative assumptions of that view of the processes of politics and government. Yet, that assumption is often thought not to hold as the rigidities of budgeting seem more and more out of step with the fluidities of political life in those societies. Our research suggests, however, that the mainstay of that linkage is less the vitality of any one political institution and more the vitality of political parties and interest groups whose conflicts and compromises underlie the workings of those institutions.

The acceptance by higher reviewing levels of lower level officials' initiations of change is closely linked to the stances of various political parties. The higher the level of support for agency activities by each political party, the more successful the agency in obtaining requested budget increases and in expanding expenditure bases over time. A substantial number of these officials in Oslo have told us that members of political parties, both leaders and elected representatives, have frequently initiated contacts with higher level reviewing agents in support of agency budget requests. Furthermore, members of political parties hold formal positions on a number of governmental structures which provide them with additional opportunities for influence on budgeting.

Lest we present a view of resource allocation processess so volatile as to belie the marked stability clearly evidenced in much of public budgeting, we need to emphasize two points. First, we are speaking explicitly of change in budgeting and not of the sizeable portions of public budgets which remain stable year after year. Certainly partisan efforts to introduce more dramatic change in the constants of budgeting would need to be more massive indeed. Second, parties do not react to all initiations of change at lower levels, but only to those changes immersed in political controversy. The more controversial the activities of the agency, the higher the probability of intervention and contact by the several political parties.

This heightened activism of political parties on matters of resource allocation is not devoid of the content of dominant political, social, and ideological cleavages in societies. In other words, party activism on budgetary questions is not a game of power insulated from the dimensions of conflict which have always separated each party from the other. The most enduring dimension of political conflict in Norwegian society over the years has been the left-right dimension of government involvement in the economic and social life of Norwegian society; and the seven political parties have exhibited much unidimensional variance on that issue ranging from the views of the Communist Party on the left to those of the Conservative Party on the right.

That dimension of conflict is very much reflected in the patterns of partisan support and opposition for different agencies in budgeting. Parties on the left tend to be quite similar in terms of the agencies to which they afford support and opposition on expenditure issues but quite different from the bourgeois parties on the right. Furthermore, the ordering of these parties along such a dimension appears quite consistent with our intuitive judgments of the ideological proclivities of these parties and with other analyses based on mass electoral evaluations.

Parties on the left seem particularly likely to intervene at various decision points on budgetary issues. It may be that at least some portion of the explanation for the rapidly expanding role of government in these societies lies in the differential commitments to activism by those who would accelerate change and those who would retard it. If parties of the left are more active in supporting change, they may be more successful in inducing it. This does not mean, however, that minority bourgeois parties will become irrelevant on important questions of financial resource allocation. Statistically, we increase our level of explanation by significant quantities when we include the support of opposition of these minority bourgeois parties in Oslo.

Change in the patterns of financial resource allocation seem closely tied to the viewpoints, preferences, and activities of political parties. Yet, we never imagined that such a view would constitute the only theoretically plausible explanation for the relevance of politics for budgeting. We have examined an alternative explanation – the view that success and change in budgeting is a function of the level of support or opposition from alternative structures in government. Particularly from the standpoint of the multiplicity of competing and interacting structures within modern governments, the expectation that budgeting outcomes would become increasingly dependent on the conflicts, compromises, and support among alternative competing structures seemed especially promising.

We do not find much support for that explanation, however, if we carry its components to their logical conclusion. Certainly, one implication is that consistent views about governmental activity come to characterize each structure or its members; and one is led to make such statements as 'the Council finance committee supports a given change while the City Cabinet is in opposition.' Such a pattern would presumably be accompanied by the demise of previously dominant political cleavages manifested through the activities and interventions of political parties and interest groups. In contrast, however, our analyses suggest that important structures in government, while obviously central to the resolution of conflict in budgeting, provide settings in which more customary and enduring dimensions of conflict manifest themselves. Members of political parties certainly hold formal positions on many of these structures; but the saliency of partisan conflict remains; and the structures become vehicles through which party effects on budgeting may be felt.

Elements internal to the party systems do not, however, constitute the full set of influences on the directions of budgetary change. Dominant interest groups in societies are particularly likely to show strong systematic effects at stages in the process of budgetary review. While interest groups seem to show slight or insignificant input into agency budget requests, their impact at higher reviewing levels on the direction and acceptance of change is more dramatic. Relevant interest groups are especially active in contacting higher reviewing agents in support of agency attempts at budget expansion. Agencies may request what they will; but it seems clear that support for those requests by an array of interest groups, willing to contact important administrative and political leaders, holds substantial payoffs in terms of final acceptance of requested budgetary changes.

There are a number of explanations for the differences in our findings and interpretations for budgeting in a Scandinavian city and those from other studies of budgeting in other settings – variations in research design, our explicit focus on change, Oslo as an historical accident, differences in national context, and so on. We cannot resolve these issues here, but we do want to suggest what is, in our view, the most promising view of those contrasts. The manipulatability, vitality, and dynamism of important decision processes within governments are only as strong as the elements outside which are supposed to control them. Given a deterministic, insulated, self-perpetuating decision-making system, no amount of tinkering to improve responsiveness will have its intended impact if the malaise of the governmental process within is a reflection of the malaise of political life outside. Where dominant interests in society are not well organized and activated in the form of groups, then their input into important governmental decision processes will be trivial. Where political parties do not represent the dominant dimensions of cleavages in societies and differences between them appear slight, then their desire and ability to shape important government decisions will be diminished. Under these conditions, the process quite naturally becomes insulated, isolated, internally deterministic, and perhaps excessively stable and resistant to change.

This may well be one of the real distinctions between budgeting in urban Scandinavia and budgeting in urban America. Urban budgeting in America may indeed be more deterministic, since it is set, in the broader context, in a society in which important interests often go unrepresented, and important dimensions of economic and social conflict are often unreflected in the policies and programs of the two dominant political parties. Indeed, the nonpartisanship of politics in many American cities further exaggerates that pattern. In such a context, it is not surprising that important decision-making processes in government seem far removed from important elements of interest and partisan politics in society.

We often speak of socialist and bourgeois parties in Europe but of two bourgeois parties in America. In European systems with more responsible parties, likely to divide more clearly on dimensions which reflect dominant cleavage issues in European societies, the potential for significant effects of politics on government decision is greater. In such a context, budgeting – as one of the most important elements of governmental decision processes – comes to reflect the vitality and dynamism of the prevailing political order in those societies.

Notes

INTRODUCTION

1 Paul E. Green and Yoram Wind, *Multiattribute Decisions in Marketing: A Measurement Approach* (Hinsdale, Illinois: The Dryden Press, 1973).
2 Tore Hansen and Francesco Kjellberg, 'Municipal Expenditures in Norway: Autonomy and Constraints in Local Government Activity', *Policy and Politics*, 4 (1976), 25–50.

CHAPTER II

1 Here we use the term 'state' in the sense that the term 'state of nature' is used in the game theoretic literature. R. Duncan Luce and Howard Raiffa, *Games and Decisions* (New York: John Wiley and Sons, Inc., 1957).
2 For those familiar with the Scandinavian languages, the following English-Norwegian translations may be helpful: agency chief-etatsjef; department head-rådmann; Chief Municipal Administrator-Finansrådmann; City Council-Bystyret. A suitable translation for finsnrådmann proved to be particularly difficult. Some may prefer the translation, Head of the Finance Department of Budget Director. While these terms are closer to a literal translation, they are misleading in terms of the functions actually performed. The scope of the Finansrådmann's activities is quite close to that for the American city manager. In any event, the scope of those activities is definitely broader than would be suggested by either of the alternative terms above. In addition, our translation is the official English translation used by the Finansrådmann's Office.
3 These data were taken from the following budget documents published by the Oslo municipal government: Sak IA: Finansrådmannens Forslag til Driftsbudsjett and Dokument nr. 3: Oslo Bykasses Driftsbudsjett, editions for 1953 through 1974.
4 Abraham Kaplan, *The Conduct of Inquiry* (San Francisco: Chandler Publishing Company, 1964), p. 198.
5 We do not mean to imply that formal representation of interest groups on governmental structure never occurs. There are specific cases in Norwegian governmental arrangements where such representation has been explicitly provided for. But, by and large, the bulk of interest groups in most societies must content themselves with influence attempts of a more informal nature.

CHAPTER III

1 Fred W. Riggs, *Administration in Developing Countries – The Theory of Prismatic Society* (Boston: Houghton Mifflin Company, 1964).
2 Milton J. Esman, 'The Politics of Development Administration', in John D. Montgomery and William J. Siffin (eds.), *Approaches to Development: Politics,*

Administration and Change (New York: McGraw-Hill Book Company, 1966), p. 59
3 Ferrel Heady, *Public Administration: A Comparative Perspective* (Englewood Cliffs, N.J.: Prentice-Hall, Inc., 1966), p. 25.
4 Thomas R. Dye, *Politics, Economics, and the Public: Policy Outcomes in the American States* (Chicago: Rand McNally and Company, 1966), Chapter II.
5 B. Guy Peters, 'Economic and Political Effects on the Development of Social Expenditures in France, Sweden and the United Kingdom', *Midwest Journal of Political Science,* (May, 1972); J. Alt, 'Some Social and Political Correlates of County Borough Expenditures', *British Journal of Political Science,* (January, 1971); Noel Boaden, *Urban Policy Making: Influences on County Boroughs in England and Wales;* Michael Aiken and Roger Depre, 'Politics and Policy Output: A Study of City Expenditures Among 196 Belgian Cities', mimeo, 1974.
6 For an alternative method of handling this problem with aggregated environmental and expenditure data for administrative units, see Andrew T. Cowart, 'Expanding Formal Models of Budgeting to Include Environmental effects', *Policy and Politics* (December, 1975).
7 Elihu Katz and Brenda Danet (eds., *Bureaucracy and the Public: A Reader in Official-Client Relations* (New York: Basic Books, Inc., Publishers, 1973).
8 David B. Truman, *The Governmental Process* (New York: Alfred A. Knopf, Inc., 1951); and Harmon Zeigler, *Interest Groups in American Society* (Englewood Cliffs, N.J.: Prentice-Hall, Inc., 1964).
9 John P. Crecine, *Governmental Problem-Solving: A Computer Simulation of Municipal Budgeting* (Chicago: Rand McNally and Company, 1969), Chapter XII.
10 Johan P. Olsen, 'Local Budgeting, Decision Making or Ritual Act', *Scandinavian Political Studies,* 5 (1970), pp. 85–113.
11 Crecine, 1969; Olsen, 1970.

CHAPTER IV

1 A Report of the Committee on Political Parties, *Toward a More Responsible Two-Party System* (Washington, D. C.: The American Political Science Association, 1950).
2 V. O. Key, Jr., *Politics, Parties, and Pressure Groups,* 4th edition (New York: Crowell, 1958).
3 Dye, *Politics, Economics, and the Public.*
4 Boaden, *Urban Policy Making: Influences on County Boroughs in England and Wales.*
5 Wildavsky, *The Politics of the Budgetary Process.*
6 See, for example, Richard F. Fenno, Jr., *The Power of the Purse: Appropriations Politics in Congress* (Boston: Little, Brown and Company, 1966).
7 Philip E. Converse and Henry Valen, 'Dimensions of Clevage and Perceived Party Distances in Norwegian Voting', *Scandinavian Political Studies,* 1971, pp. 107–152.
8 J. B. Kruskal, 'Multidimensional Scaling: A Numerical Method', *Psychometrika,* 1964, pp. 1–27; J. B. Kruskal, 'Multidimensional Scaling by Optimizing Goodness of Fit to a Nonmetric Hypothesis', *Psychometrika,* 1964, pp. 115–129; George B. Rabinowitz, 'An Introduction to Nonmetric Multidimensional Scaling', *American Journal of Political Science,* Vol. XIX, 2, (May, 1975) pp. 313–322.
9 Input measures of similarity are Pearson product-moment correlation coefficients. The stress or goodness of fit for the solution is a good-fair .08.

CHAPTER V

1 Richard F. Fenno, Jr., *The Power of the Purse*.
2 J. B. Kruskal, 'Multidimensional Scaling: A Numerical Method', *Psychometrika*, 1964, pp. 1–27; J. B. Kruskal, 'Multidimensional Scaling by Optimizing Goodness of Fit to a Nonmetric Hypothesis', *Psychometrika*, 1964, pp. 115–129.
3 The stress or goodness of fit for the solution is an excellent .002.

CHAPTER VI

1 Respondents were asked to fill in a matrix indicating the frequency ('often', 'occasionally', 'seldom', 'never') with higher level agency personnel participated in meetings on budget issues with the following: (1) internal agency personnel, (2) department head, (3) Chief Municipal Administrator, (4) Mayor, (5) layman political committee, and (6) City Council.
2 The literature on causal modelling and path analysis is now extensive. For perhaps the best compilation of readings on the subject, see H. M. Blalock, Jr. (ed.), *Causal Models in the Social Sciences* (Chicago: Aldine-Atherton, Inc., 1971).
3 James D. Barber, *Power in Committees: An Experiment in the Governmental Process* (Chicago: Rand McNally and Company), Chapter 2.

CHAPTER VII

1 Davis, Dempster, and Wildavsky, p. 530.
2 Davis, Dempster, and Wildavsky.
3 A fairly comprehensive review and discussion of the postwar economic development in Norway has been published by the Norwegian Central Bureau of Statistics under the title *The Norwegian Post-War Economy*, SØS 12 (Oslo, 1965). We have also benefited from publications by the Municipal Office of Statistics, particularly, the *Statistical Yearbook for the City of Oslo*.
4 In each case we assume the initial basis of calculation to be consistent with the notion of process incrementalism – i.e., based initially upon the decision taken immediately prior in the process. This notion of an initial basis of calculation implies that there is one figure which serves as the fundamental basis of judgment. Subsequent alterations in that initial judgment appear as additional variables in the models and contribute to the final judgment for the decision in question.
5 The equation is presented in Table 1d in a form for which the interpretation is more straightforward, given the kind of behavior it attempts to model. The actual estimation equation is of the form:
$w_t = \alpha_8 z_{t-1} + \alpha_9 (y-w)_{t-1} + \alpha_{10}(\Omega(y-w))_{t-1} + e_t$
6 For treatments of estimation methods in regression models, see: John Johnston, *Econometric Methods* (New York: McGraw-Hill, 1963); Carl F. Christ, *Econometric Models and Methods* (New York: Wiley and Sons, 1966).
7 J. Durbin and G. S. Watson, 'Testing for Serial Correlation in Least-squares Regression', part I, *Biometrika*, 37 (December, 1950), 409–428; part II, *Biometrika*, 38 (June, 1951), 159–178.
8 Similar criteria were used in the Davis, Dempster, and Wildavsky work cited above, except that the use of tests of significance for the constant term was not indicated in the published report.
9 These data were taken from the following budget documents published by the Oslo municipal government: *Sak IA: Finanstradmannens Forslag til Driftsbudsjett and Dokument nr. 3: Oslo Bykasses Driftsbudsjett*, editions for 1953 through 1971.

10 A list, by agency, of all estimated equations actually selected may be obtained from the authors upon request.
11 Sharkansky, 'Agency Requests', pp. 1230–1231.
12 See, for example, Richard Fenno, *The Power of the Purse*, chapters 10–12 (Boston and Toronto: Little, Brown, 1966).
13 Davis, Dempster, and Wildavsky, 'A Theory of the Budgetary Process', p. 530.
14 It is important to note that, while there is some variation across the six questions, this is by and large an individual phenomenon. That is, respondents found in the don't know category on one question are likely to be found in that category on other questions as well.

CHAPTER VIII

1 Aaron Wildavsky, *The Politics of the Budgetary Process* (Boston: Little, Brown and Company, 1974) p. 15.
2 Otto A. Davis, M. A. H. Dempster, and Aaron Wildavsky, 'Toward a Predictive Theory of Government Expenditures', *British Journal of Political Science*, 1974.
3 Johan P. Olsen, 'Local Budgeting, Decision Making or Ritual Act', *Scandinavian Political Studies*, 5 (1970) pp. 85–113.
4 John P. Crecine, *Governmental Problem-Solving: A Computer Simulation of Municipal Budgeting* (Chicago: Rand McNally and Company, 1969).